Streeteze

C000224969

Key to street plans
Allwedd i blaniau stryd

Plans drawn at a scale of 4 inches to 1 mile
Aruluniwyd y planiau yn ôl y raddfa 4 modfedd i 1 filltir

M4	Motorway	*Traffordd*
A48	A road (Trunk road)	*Ffordd A (Priffordd)*
A48	Dual carriageway	*Ffordd ddeuol*
B4281	B road	*Ffordd B*
	Through road	*Ffordd drwodd*
- - - - - -	Track/Footpath	*Llwybr/Llwybr troed*
-·-·-·-	County boundary	*Ffin sirol*
-··-··-	Municipal boundary	*Ffin fwrdeisiol*
▬▬▬	Railway	*Rheilffordd*
░░░	Woods and forest	*Coedtir a choedwig*

P	Car parks (major)	*(prif) Maes parcio*
☉✝✡	Places of worship	*Mannau addoliad*
🏨🍺	Hotel/Public house	*Gwesty/Tafarndy*
🛢	Petrol station	*Gorsaf betrol*
🔔	Police station	*Gorsaf heddlu*
✉	Post Office	*Swyddfa'r Post*
M 🎭	Theatre/Museum	*Theatr/Amgueddfa*
T	Toilet facility	*Cyfleustra toiled*
➕	Health centre	*Canolfan iechyd*
🚐	Caravan site	*Safleoedd carafannau*

1 A B C D

1 2 3 4 5 6

INDEX TO MAPS ON PAGES 1-6

cont.

KEY TO MAPS ON PAGES 1-6

▬▬▬ Motorway	▬ · ▬ County boundary
▬▬▬ A road	▦ Urban areas
▬▬▬ B road	o o Towns/villages
▬▬▬ Through road	0 1 2 Miles
▬▬▬ Dual carriageway	0 1 2 3 Kilometres

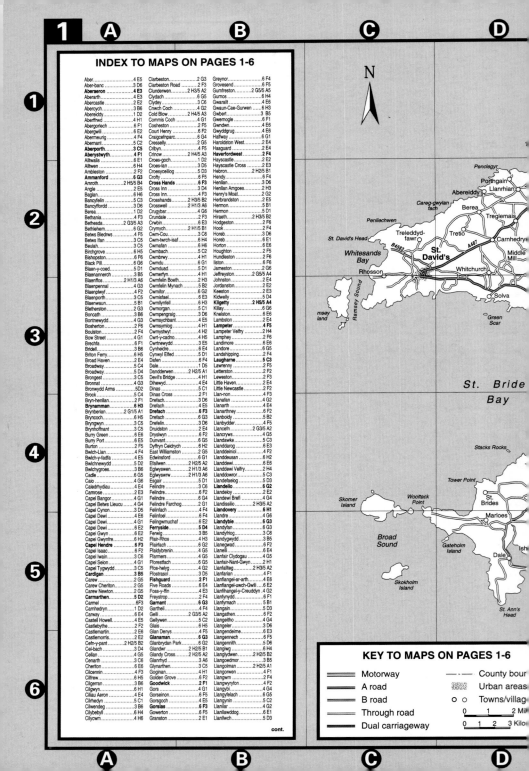

N

Panclegyr
Porthgain
Abereiddy
Llanrhian
Careg-gwylan-fach
Berea
Treglemais
Penllechwen
Treleddyd-fawr
Tretio
Carnhedryn
St. David's Head
B4583
Whitesands Bay
St. David's
A487
Middle Mill
Ramsey Sound
Whitchurch
Rhosson
Solva
Imsey Island
Green Scar
St. Bride Bay
Stacks Rocks
Tower Point
Skomer Island
Wooltack Point
St. Brides
Marloes
Broad Sound
Gateholm Island
Dale
Ish
Skokholm Island
St. Ann's Head

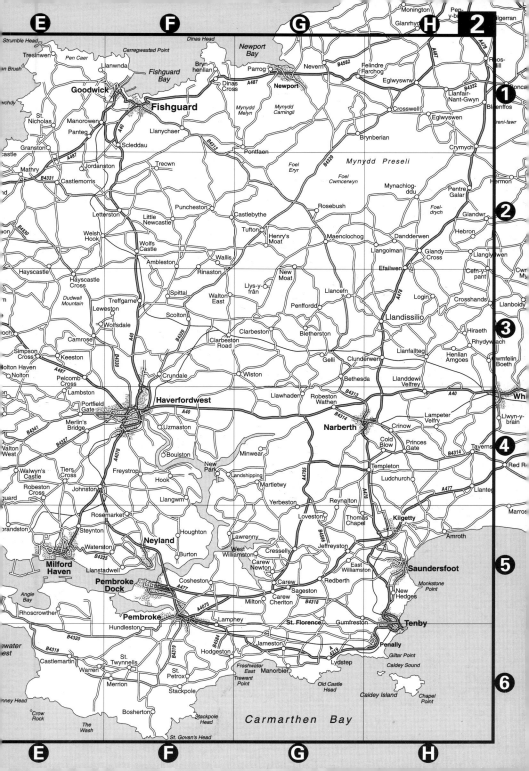

Index (continued)

Place	Ref	Place	Ref
Llanllwni	4 E6	Martletwy	2 G4
Llanmadoc	6 E6	Mathry	2 E2
Llanmiloe	5 C4	Meidrim	5 C2
Llanmorlais	6 F5	Merlin's Bridge	2 E4
Llannon	4 E5	Merrion	2 F6
Llanpumsaint	5 D1	Merthyr	5 D2
Llanrhian	1 D2	Middle Mill	1 D2
Llanrhidian	6 E6	**Milford Haven**	**2 E5**
Llanrhystud	4 F2	Minwear	2 G4
Llansadurnen	5 C4	Monachty	2 F1
Llansamlet	6 F6	Monington	3 A5
Llansantffraed	4 E3	Morfa Bach	5 D3
Llansawel	4 G6	Morriston	6 G5
Llanstadwell	2 F5	Moylgrove	3 A5
Llanstephan	**5 D4**	Myddfai	6 H1
Llanteg	2 H4/5 B4	Mydroilyn	4 E4
Llanwenog	4 E5	Mynachlog-ddu	2 H2/5 A1
Llanwnio	5 C2	Nanternis	3 D4
Llanwrda	2 E1	Nantgaredig	6 E3
Llanwnnen	4 F5	Nantycaws	6 E3
Llanwrda	6 H1	**Narberth**	**2 G4/5 A3**
Llanybri	5 C3	Neath	6 H5
Llanynog	2 F1	Nebo	4 F3
Llanychaer	5 C3	Nevern	2 G1/3 A6
Llawhaden	2 G4	New Hedges	2 H5/5 A4
Llechryd	3 B5	New Inn	4 E6
Lledrod	4 G2	New Moat	2 G2
Lidiad-Nenog	4 F4	New Park	2 F4
Llundain-fach	4 F4	**New Quay**	**3 D4**
Llwyn-y-brain	5 B3	**Newcastle Emlyn**	**3 C6**
Llwyn-y-groes	4 F4	Newchapel	3 B6
Llwyncelyn	4 E4	Newchurch	5 D2
Llwyndafydd	3 D4	Newgale	2 E3
Llys-y-frân	2 G3	**Newport**	**2 G1**
Login	2 H3/5 A2	Newton	6 F6
Loughor	6 F5	**Neyland**	**2 F5**
Loveston	2 G5/5 A4	Nicholaston	6 F6
Ludchurch	2 H4/5 A3	Nolton	2 E3
Lydstep	2 G6/5 A5	Nolton Haven	2 E3
Maenclochog	2 G2/5 A1	Oakford	4 E4
Maescrugiau	4 E6	Oxwich	6 E6
Maesllyn	3 D5	Pant-lasau	6 G5
Maesybont	6 F3	Panteg	2 E1
Manorbier	2 G6	Pantglas Hall	6 F2
Manordeilo	6 G2	Pantgwyn	3 B5
Manorowen	2 E1	Parc-Henri	6 F2
Margam	6 H6	Parcllyn	3 B4
Marloes	1 D5	Parkmill	6 F6
Marros	5 B4		

Place	Ref	Place	Ref
Parrog	2 G1	Ponterwyd	4 H1
Pelcomb Cross	2 E3	Pontfaen	2 G1
Pembrey	5 D5	Pontgarreg	3 D4
Pembroke	**2 F5**	Ponthirwaun	3 C5
Pembroke Dock	**2 F5**	Pontlliw	6 G5
Pen-bont	2 G1	Pontrhydfendigaid	4 H3
Pen-y-banc	6 G2	Pontrhydyfen	6 H5
Pen-y-bont	5 C2	Pontyates	6 E4
Pen-y-bryn	3 B6	**Pontyberem**	**6 E3**
Pen-y-garn	6 F1	Port Eynon	6 E6
Pen-y-groes	**6 F3**	Port Talbot	6 H6
Penally	**2 H6/5 A5**	Portfield Gate	2 E4
Penant	4 E3	Porthgain	1 D2
Penbryn	3 C4	Porthyrhyd	4 H6
Pencader	4 E6	Princes Gate	2 H4/5 A3
Pencarreg	4 F5	Pumpsaint	4 G6
Penclawdd	6 F5	Puncheston	2 F2
Pendine	5 B4	Pwll	6 E5
Penffordd	2 G3	Pwll-trap	5 C3
Penherder	3 C6	Red Roses	5 B3
Penllergaer	6 G5	Redberth	2 G5/5 A4
Penman	6 F6	Reynalton	2 G5/5 A4
Pennard	6 F6	Reynoldston	6 E6
Penparc	3 B5	Rhadmad	4 F2
Penparcau	4 F1	Rhandirmwyn	4 H5
Penrhiw-llan	3 D6	Rhos	3 D6
Penrhiwpal	3 D5	Rhos-Hill	3 B6
Penrhiwpal	4 E6	Rhoscrowther	2 E5
Pentre Galar	2 H2/5 B1	Rhosmaen	6 G2
Pentre-Gwenlais	6 G3	Rhossili	5 D6
Pentre-bâch	4 F5	Rhosson	1 C2
Pentre-cwrt	3 D6	Rhyd-Rosser	4 F3
Pentre-llyn	4 G2	Rhyd-y-fro	6 H4
Pentrebach	2 F6	Rhydargaeau	6 E1
Pentrecagal	3 C6	Rhydcymerau	4 F6
Pentrefelin	6 F2	Rhydlewis	3 D5
Pentregat	3 D5	Rhydowen	3 D5
Penuwch	4 F3	Rhydwyrach	2 H3/5 B2
Penywern	2 E3	Rinaston	2 F2
Piwmp	3 D4	Roberston Cross	2 E4
Pont Creuddyn	4 F4	Roberston Wathen	2 G4/5 A3
Pont Henry	6 E3	Roch	2 E3
Pont Siân	4 E5	Rosebush	2 G5/5 A1
Pont-rhyd-y-groes	4 H2	Rosemarket	2 F5
Pontantwn	**6 E3**	Sageston	2 G5
Pontardawe	6 H4	Salem	4 G1
Pontardulais	6 F4	Salem	6 G2
Pontarsais	6 E1	Sandfields	6 H6

Place	Ref	Place	Ref
Sarnau	5 C2	Trapp	6 G2
Saron	**6 F3**	Tre-groes	3 D5
Saundersfoot	**2 H5/5 A4**	Trecwn	2 F2
Scleddau	2 F1	Trefenter	4 G2
Scolton	2 F3	Treffgarne	2 F3
Scurlage	6 E6	Treffynnon	2 E2
Silian	4 F5	Trefilan	4 F4
Siloh	4 H6	Trefin	1 D2
Simpson Cross	2 E3	**Tregaron**	**4 G3**
Sketty	6 G6	Treglemais	1 D2
Solva	1 C2	Treleddyd-fawr	1 C2
Southgate	6 F6	Tremain	3 B5
Spittal	2 F3	Tresaith	3 B5
Square and Compass	2 E2	Tresinwen	1 E1
St. Brides	1 D4	Tretio	1 D2
St. Clears	**5 D1**	Trimsaran	6 E4
St. David's	**1 C2**	Troedyraur	3 C5
St. Dogmaels	**3 A5**	Tufton	2 F2
St. Florence	**2 G5/5 A5**	**Tumble**	**6 F3**
St. Ishmael	5 D4	Twynllanan	6 H2
St. Ishmael's	1 D5	Ty-nant	4 E4
St. Nicholas	2 E1	**Tycroes**	**6 G4**
St. Petrox	2 F6	Tynygraig	4 H2
St. Twynnells	2 F6	Upper Cwm-twrch	6 H3
Stackpole	2 F6	Upper Killay	6 F6
Star	5 B1	Uzmaston	2 F4
Steynton	2 F5	Wallis	2 F2
Strata Florida	4 H3	Walton East	2 F3
Swansea	6 G5	Walton West	2 E4
Swyddffynnon	4 G3	Walwyn's Castle	2 E4
Sylen	6 E4	Warren	2 F6
Synod Inn	3 D4	Waterston	2 F5
Taibach	6 H5	Waunarlwydd	6 F5
Tal-sarn	4 F4	Welsh Hook	2 F2
Talbenny	1 D4	West Cross	6 G6
Talgarreg	3 D5	West Williamston	2 G5
Talley	6 G1	Whitchurch	1 C2
Talog	5 C2	**Whitland**	**5 B3**
Tan-y-groes	3 C5	Wiston	2 G3
Tavernspite	2 H4/5 B3	Wolfs Castle	2 F2
Tegryn	5 B1	Wolfsdale	2 F2
Temple Bar	4 F5	Yerbeston	2 G5
Templeton	2 H4/5 A3	Ysbyty Cynfyn	4 H1
Tenby	**2 H6/5 A5**	Ysbyty Ystwyth	4 H2
The Mumbles	6 G6	Ystalyfera	6 H4
Thomas Chapel	2 G5/5 A4	Ystrad Aeron	4 F4
Three Crosses	6 F5	Ystradmeurig	4 H3
Tiers Cross	2 E4	Ystradowen	6 H3
Tonna	6 H5		

Cardigan Bay / Bae Ceredigion

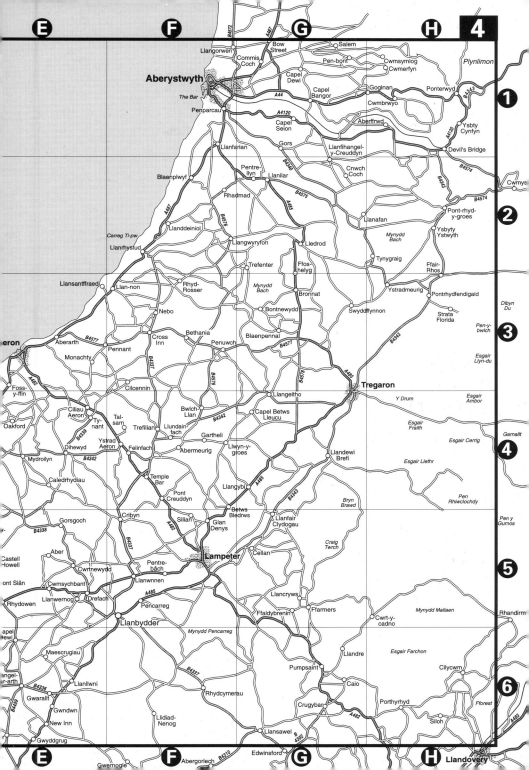

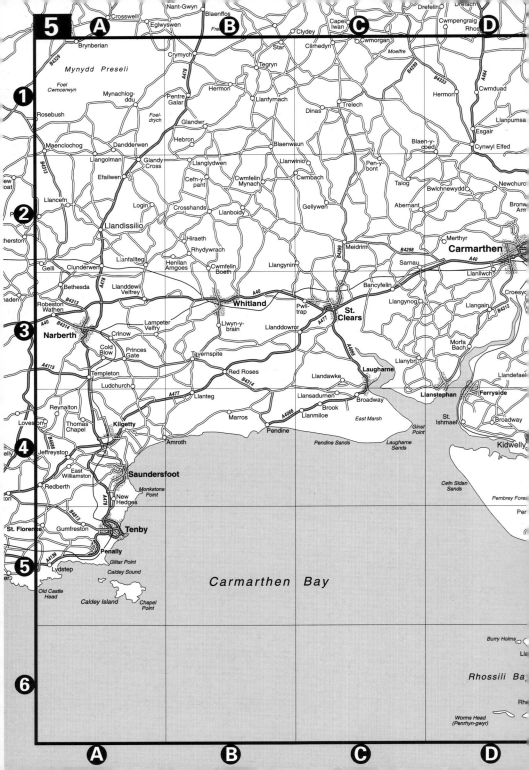

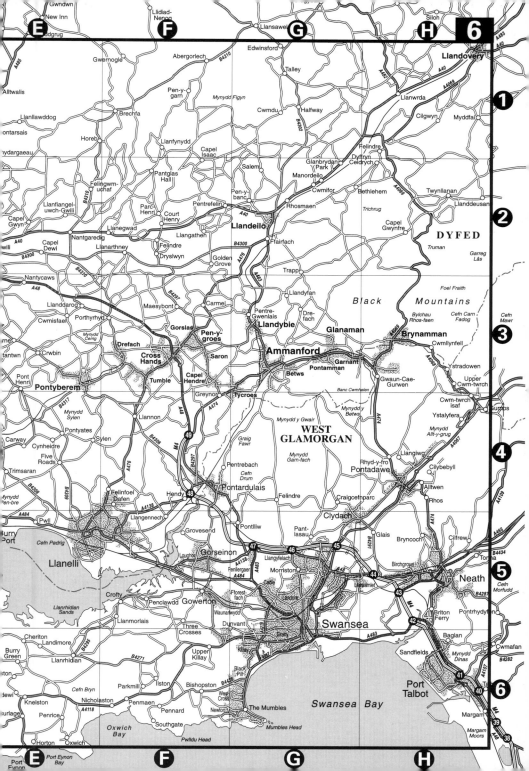

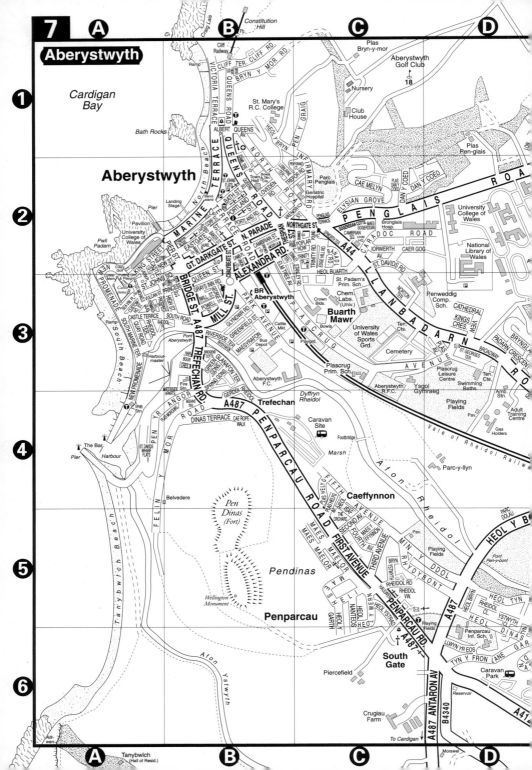

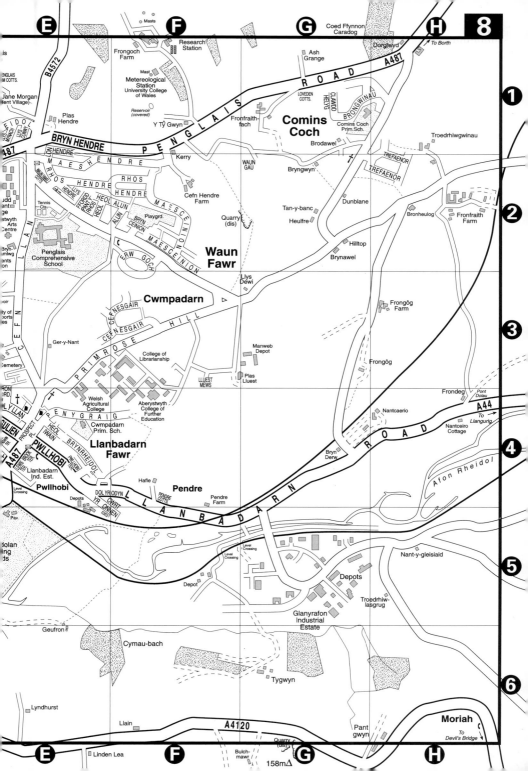

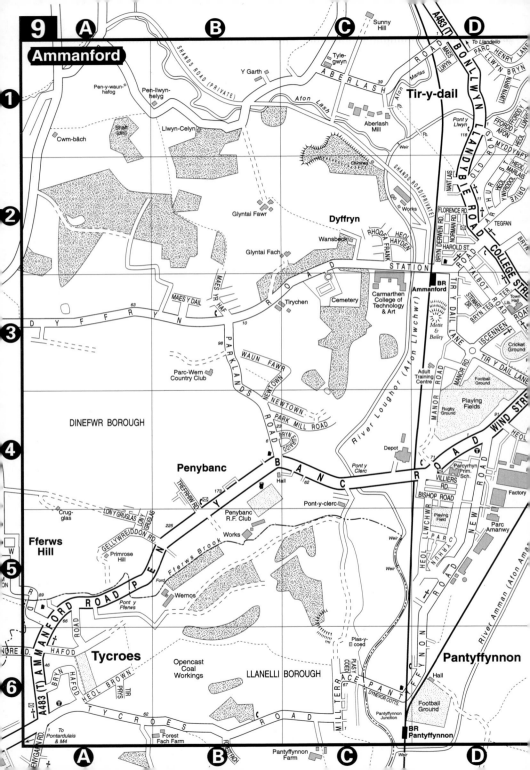

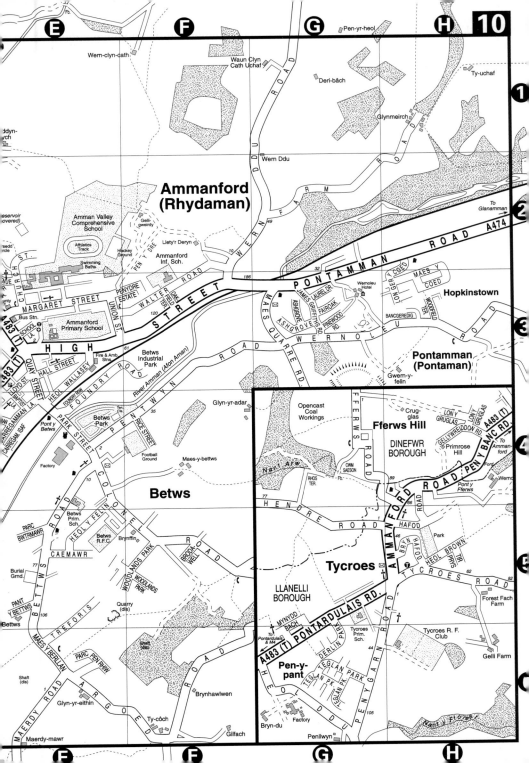

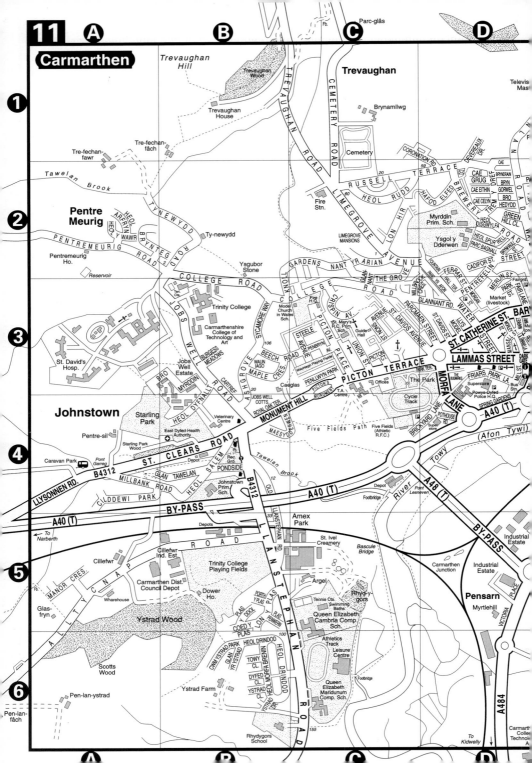

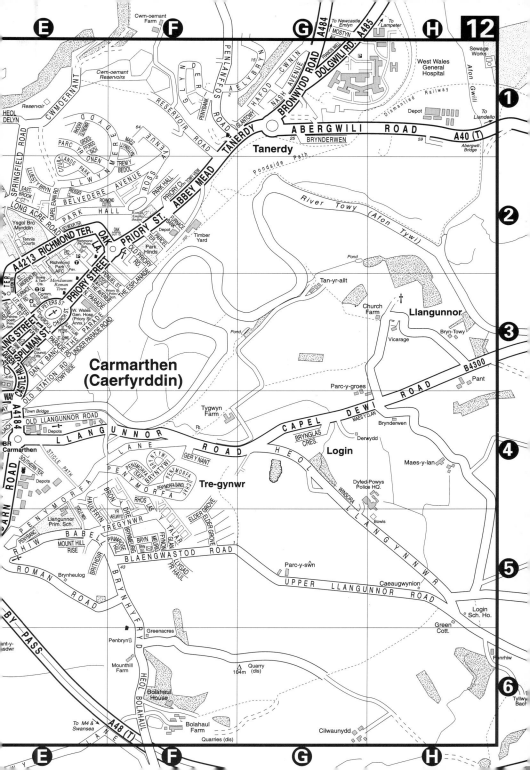

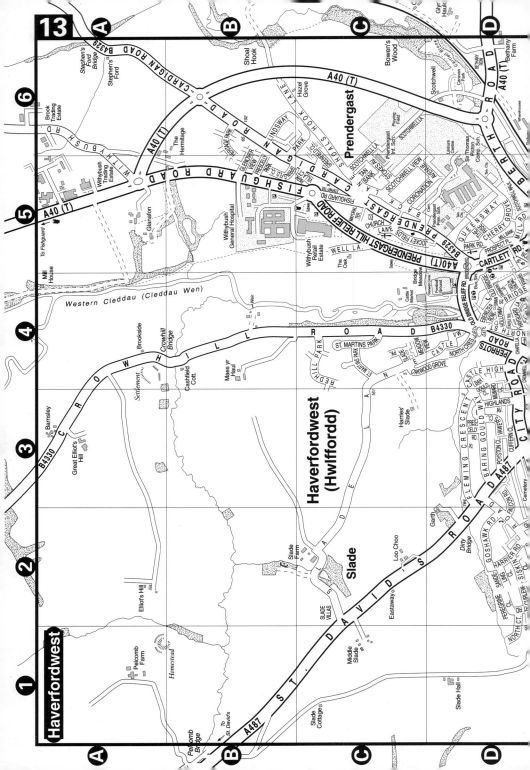

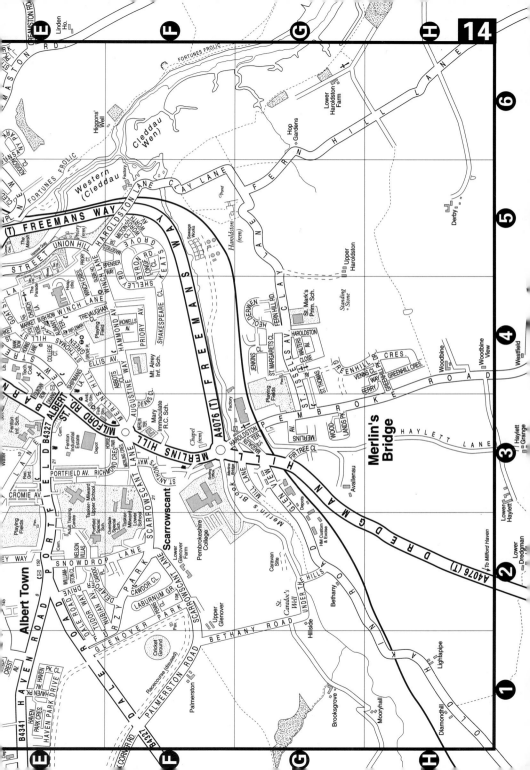

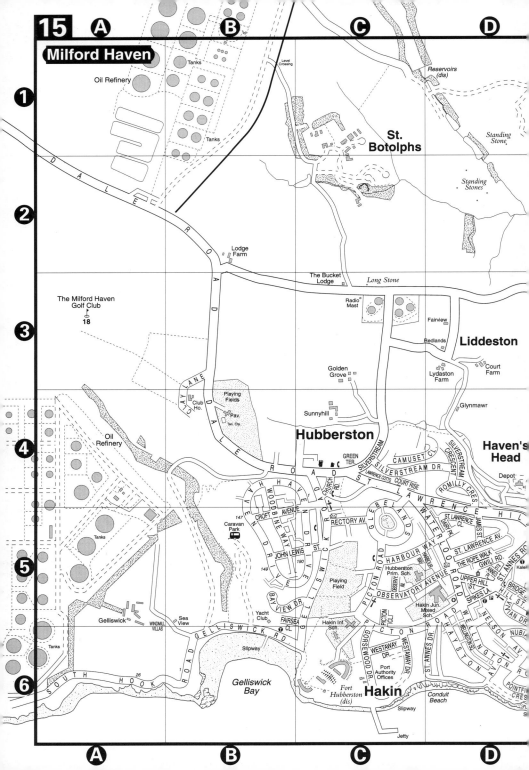

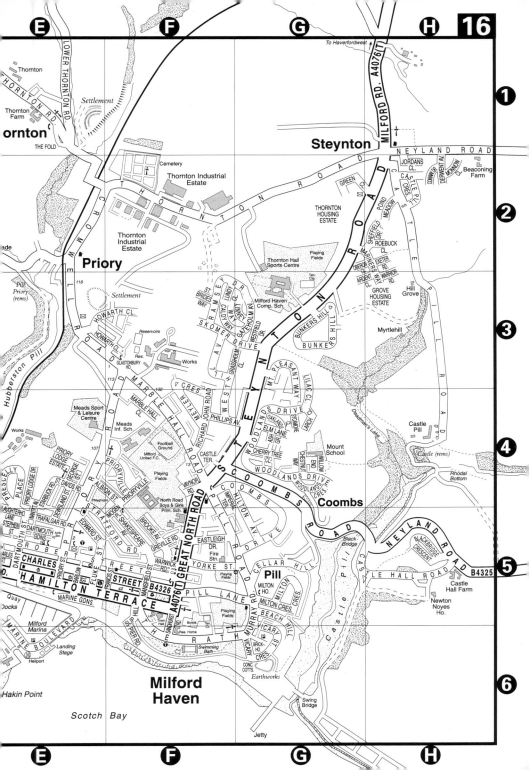

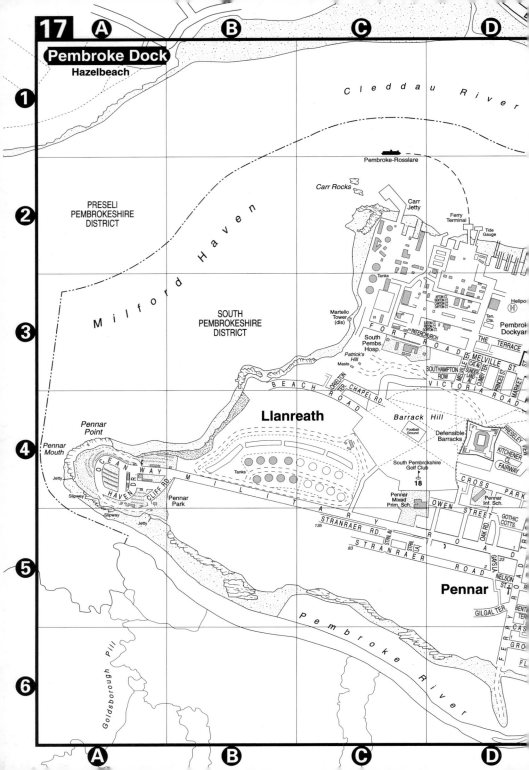

Pembroke Dock
Hazelbeach

1

Cleddau River

Pembroke-Rosslare

Carr Rocks

2

PRESELI
PEMBROKESHIRE
DISTRICT

Carr
Jetty

Ferry
Terminal

Tide
Gauge

M i l f o r d   H a v e n

Tanks

Helipo

AFTON CT.
BENTON CT.
CANTON CT.
DAYTON CT.

Ten.
Cts.

3

SOUTH
PEMBROKESHIRE
DISTRICT

Martello
Tower
(dis)

EATON CT.
PISTON CT.
PICTON CT.
DORTON CT.

F
O
R
T

R
O
A
D

PATERCHURCH

Pembrok
Dockyar

THE
TERRACE

MELVILLE
ST.

South
Pembs.
Hosp.

Patrick's
Hill

Masts

SOUTHAMPTON
ROW

VICTORIA ROAD

MARKET

PRINCESS

CUMBY TER

SUNDERLAND

EXETER

MELVILLE

BEACH   ROAD

OPRELTON TER

CHAPEL RD.

Barrack Hill

Llanreath

Football
Ground

Defensible
Barracks

PRESELI VIE

KITCHENER
CL
FAIRWAY

4

Pennar
Point

Pennar
Mouth

Tanks

South Pembrokeshire
Golf Club

18

CROSS

PARK

Jetty

O
C
E
A
N
W
A
Y

H
A
V
E
N
D
R
.

CLIFF RD.

Pennar
Park

M
I
L
I
T
A
R
Y

Pennar Mixed
Prim. Sch.

OWEN   STREET

Pennar
Inf. Sch.

GOTHIC
COTTS.

Slipway

Slipway

STRANRAER RD.
135

STRN AV.

STRN
LA.

OAK RD.

5

Jetty

STRANRAER   ROAD
83

GAS LA.

NELSON   ST.

23

FERRY ROAD

CASTE

Pennar

GILGAL TER

BENTI
TER

GRO

6

Goldsborough Pill

P e m b r o k e   R i v e r

FL

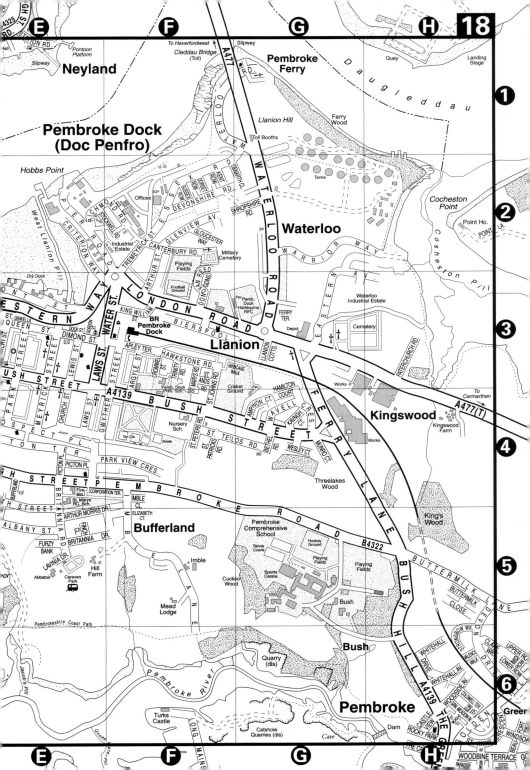

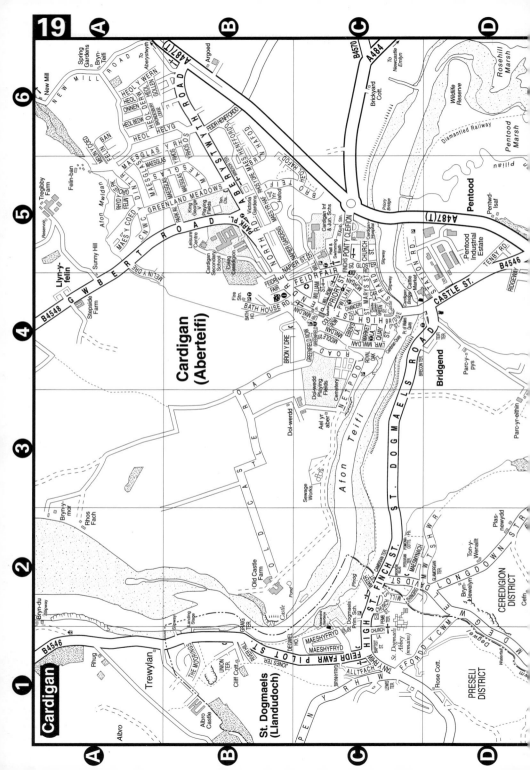

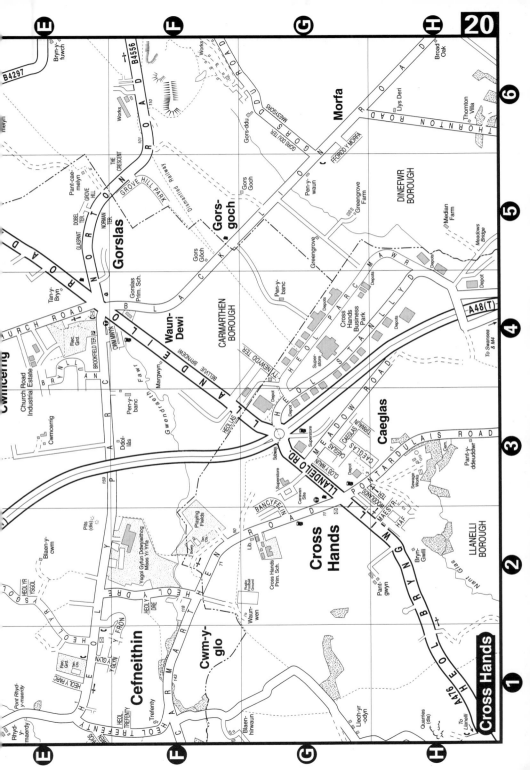

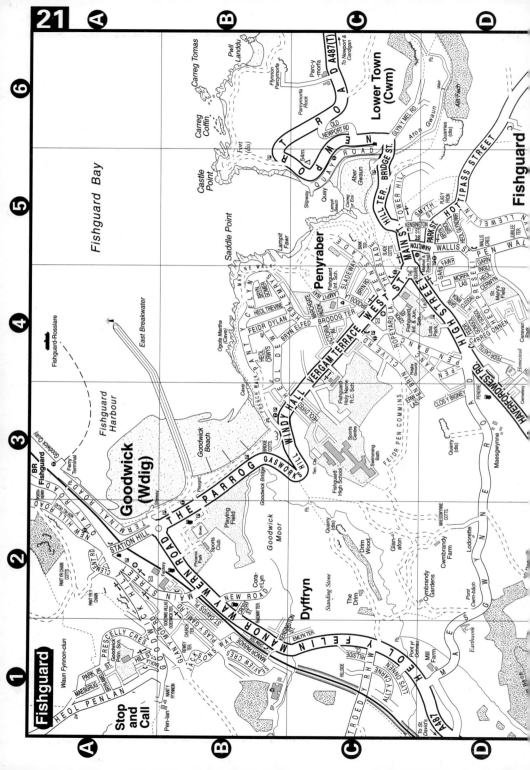

Fishguard

Fishguard

Fishguard Bay

Lower Town (Cwm)

Penyraber

Goodwick (Wdig)

Dyffryn

Stop and Call

Fishguard Harbour

Fishguard-Rosslare

East Breakwater

Goodwick Beach

Goodwick Moor

Castle Point

Saddle Point

A 487(T)

To Newport & Cardigan

To St David's

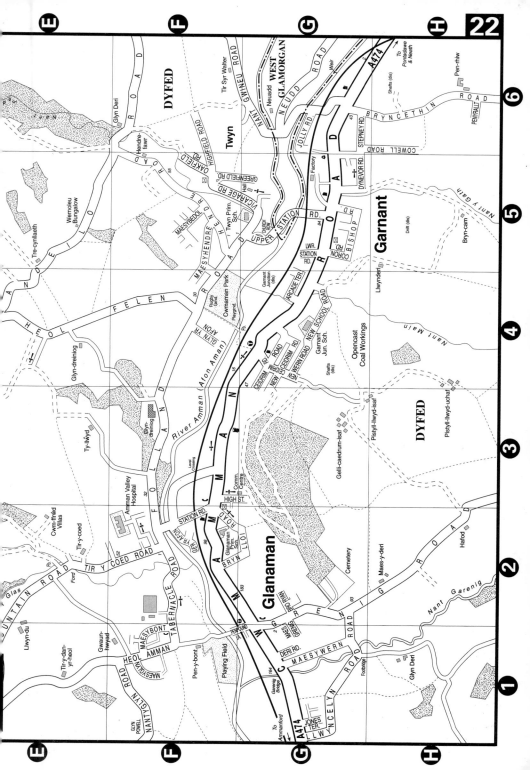

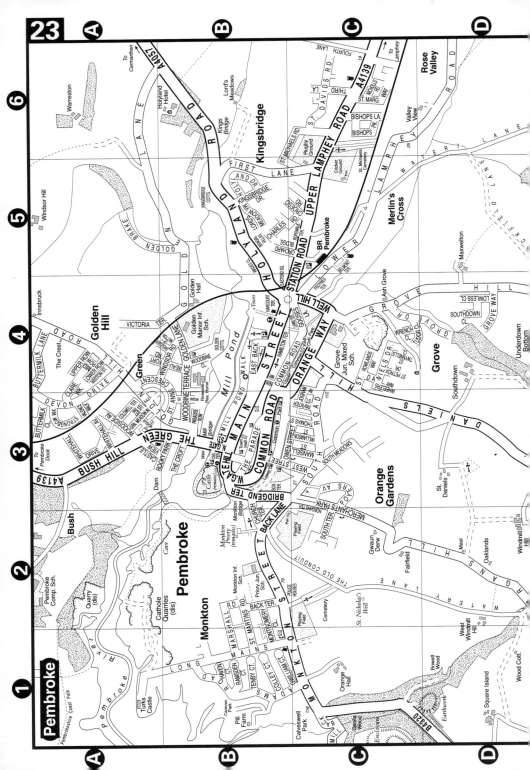

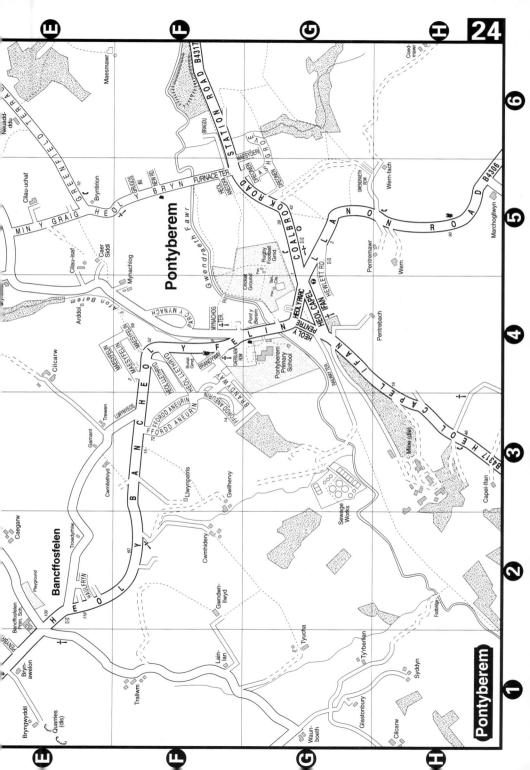

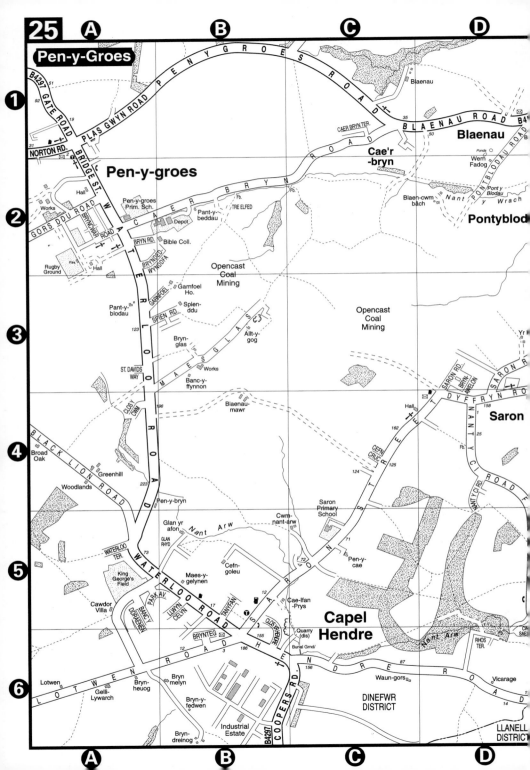

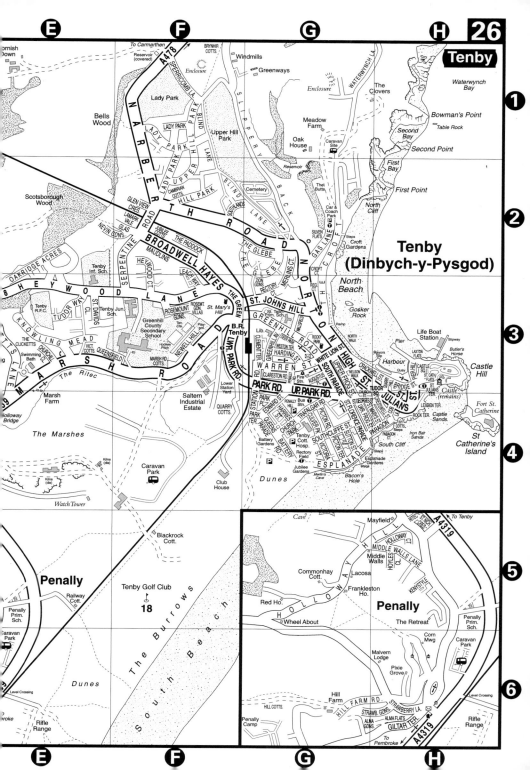

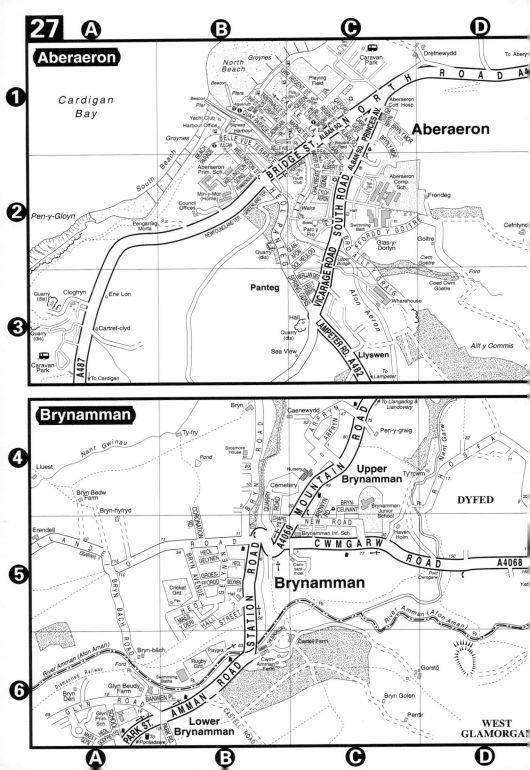

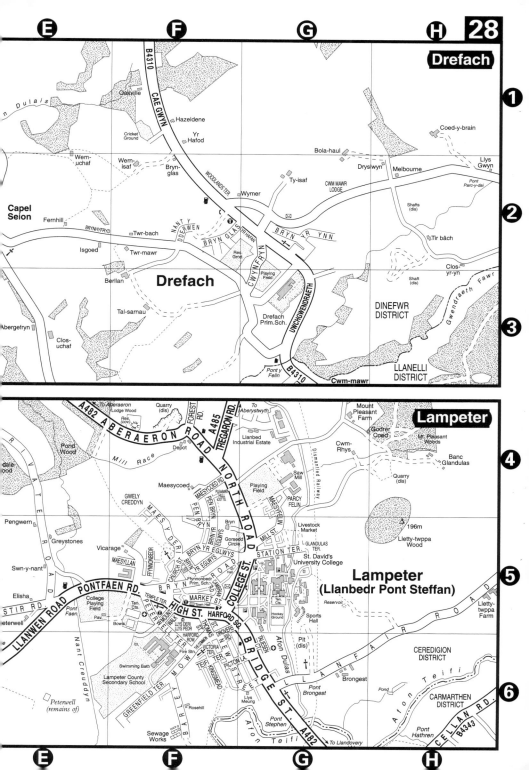

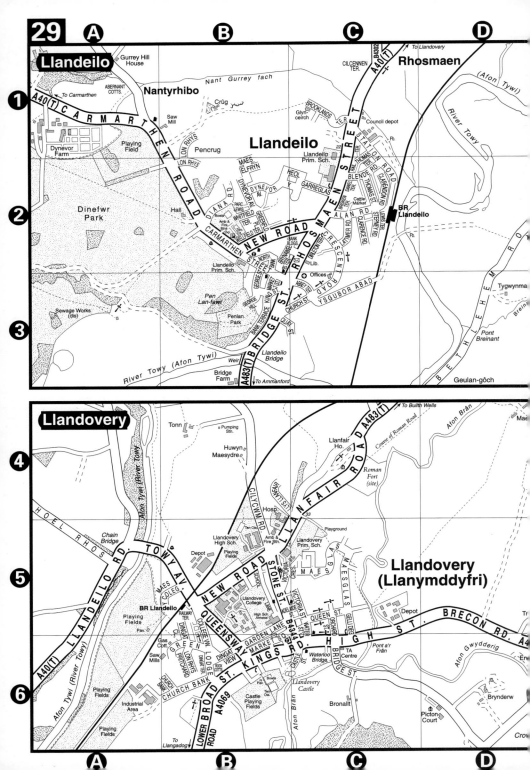

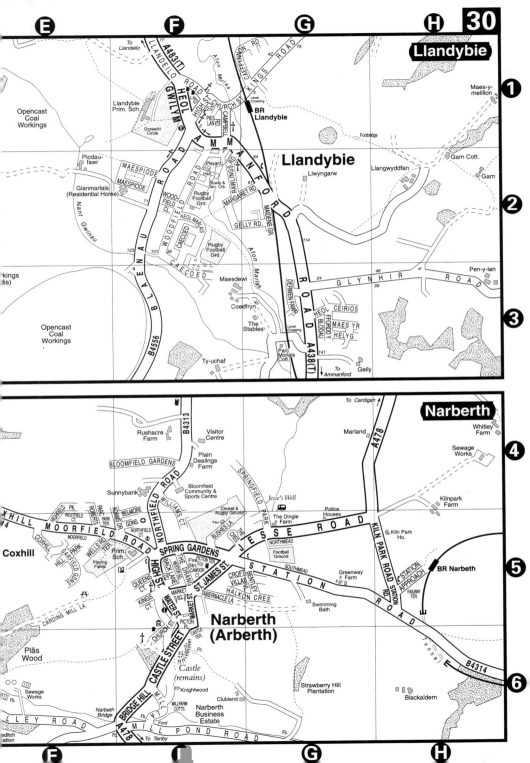

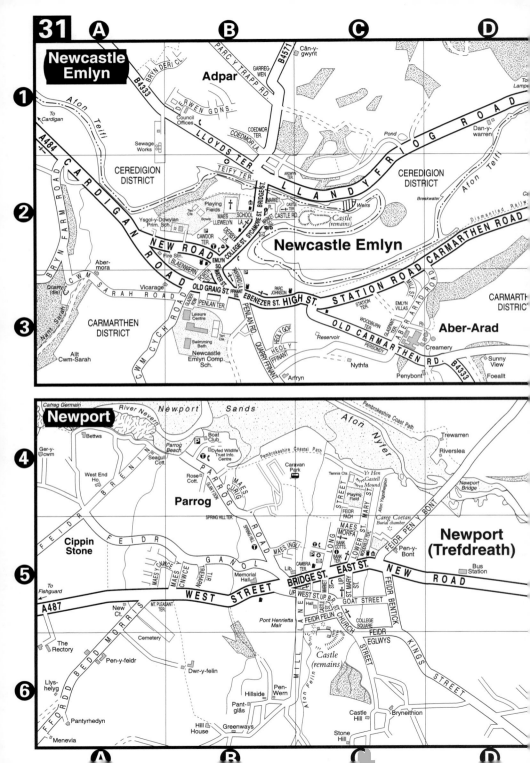

A   **B**   **C**   **D**

Newcastle Emlyn

Cân-y-gwynt

Adpar

BRYN DERI CL.

PARC Y TRAPP RD

GARREG-WEN

B4571

B4333

Afon Teifi

To Cardigan

ERWEN GDNS.

Council Offices

COEDMOR TER.

Sewage Works

LLOYDS TER.

COEDMORFA

CEREDIGION DISTRICT

TEIFY TER.

LLANDYFRIOG ROAD

Pond

Dan-y-warren

To Lampe

CEREDIGION DISTRICT

Afon Teifi

Breakwater

Dismantled Railw

Playing Fields

MAES LLEWELYN

ARDWYN TER.

MARKET PL.

BRIDGE ST.

CASTLE TER.

CASTLE RD.

Weirs

Castle (remains)

CARMARTHEN ROAD

Bowls

Ysgol-y-Ddwylan Prim. Sch.

CAWDOR TER.

DERBY LA.

COLLEGE ST.

SYCAMORE ST.

SCHOOL LA.

Newcastle Emlyn

Aber-mora

NEW ROAD

Fire Stn.

BLAENWERN

EMLYN SQ.

POTH

MARWEL LA.

PARC JOHNSON

STATION ROAD

STATION TER.

EMLYN VILLAS

ABER ARAD RD

CARMARTH DISTRIC

Quarry (dis)

CWM SARAH ROAD

Vicarage

OLD GRAIG ST.

FFYNANT SQ.

PENLAN RD.

EBENEZER ST.

HIGH ST.

WOODBURN TER.

GLASNET

Pb

Aber-Arad

CARMARTHEN DISTRICT

PENLAN TER.

QUARRY FFYNANT

HEOL GOF

Reservoir

PERSONDY

OLD CARMARTHEN RD.

Creamery

Allt Cwm-Sarah

NANT SARAH

Leisure Centre

Ten Cots.

HEOL Y FFYNANT

Sunny View

Swimming Bath

Newcastle Emlyn Comp. Sch.

Artryn

Nythfa

Penybont

B4333

Foeallt

Newcastle

Newport

Carreg Germain

River Nevern

Newport Sands

Pembrokeshire Coast Path

Afon Nyfer

Ger-y-cwm

Bettws

Boat Club

Parrog Beach

Dyfed Wildlife Trust Info. Centre

Pembrokeshire Coastal Path

Caravan Park

Trewarren

Riverslea

West End Ho.

Seagull Cott.

Rose Cott.

PARROG ROAD

MAES CURIG

BANTON

Tennis Cts.

Yr Hen Gastell Mound

STREET

MARY ST.

LONG STREET

Newport Bridge

Parrog

SPRING HILL TER.

SPRING HILL

MAES INGLI

FEIDR FACH

MAES MORFA

BANK COTTS.

CAMBRIA TER.

BANK ST.

LOWER ST.

WOODVILLE ST.

Carreg Coetan Burial chamber

FEIDR PEN BONT

Pen-y-Bont

Newport (Trefdreath)

Cippin Stone

FEIDR GANOL

TIR TREHAN

MAES CWNCE

MAES CWNCE

Memorial Hall

Lib.

EAST ST.

MARKET LANE

NEW ROAD

Bus Station

To Fishguard

A487

WEST STREET

BRIDGE ST.

UP. WEST ST.

HALL

GOAT STREET

FEIDR BENTICK

New Ct.

MT. PLEASANT TER.

MILL LANE

UP. BR.

FEIDR FELIN

CHURCH STREET

COLLEGE SQUARE

KINGS STREET

Pont Henrietta Mair

The Rectory

Cemetery

MORRIS BEDD FFORDD

Pen-y-feidr

Dwr-y-felin

Pant-glâs

Pen-Wern

Aton Felin

Castle (remains)

FEIDR EGLWYS

Llys-helyg

Hillside

Greenways

Castle Hill

Bryneithion

Pantyrhedyn

Hill House

Stone Hill

Menevia

A   **B**   **C**   **D**

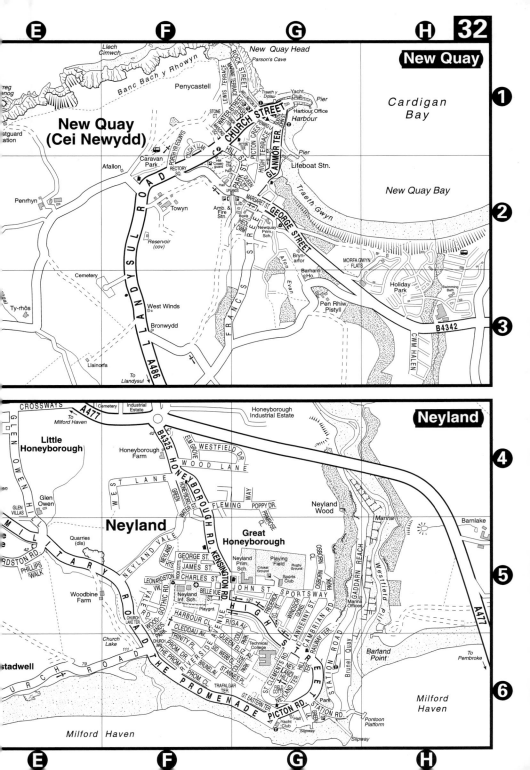

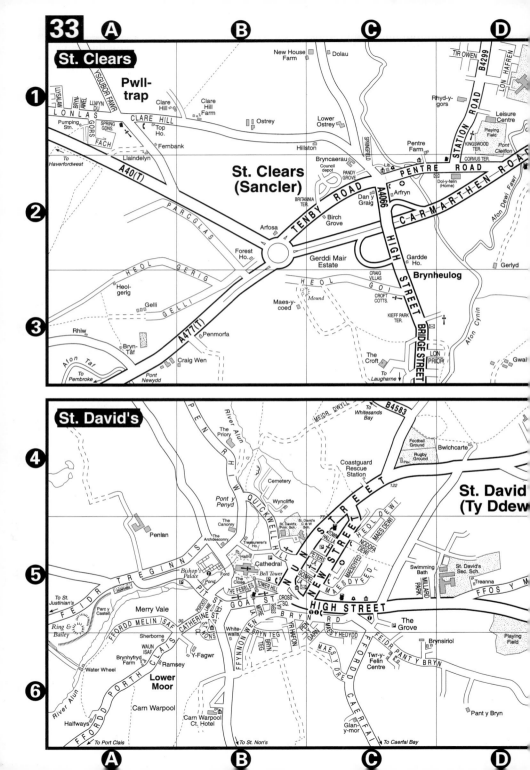

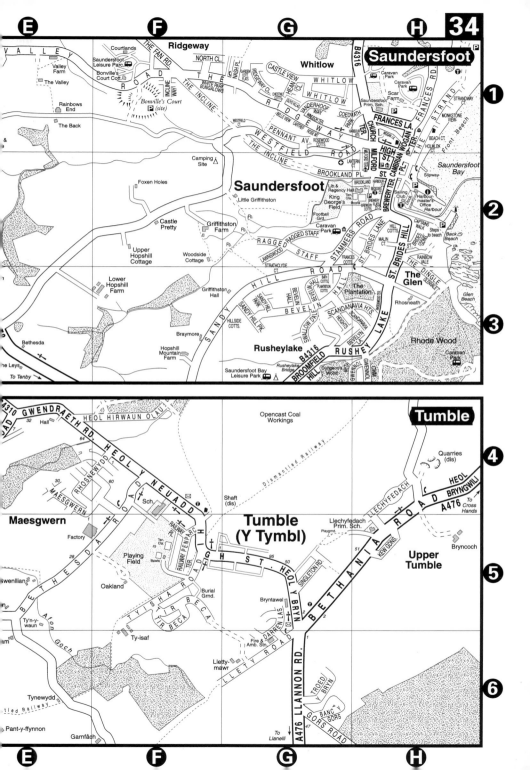

E   **F**   **G**   **H**

VALLEY

Courtlands
Ridgeway
NORTH CL.
Whitlow
Saundersfoot
B4316

THE FAN RD.

Valley Farm
Saundersfoot Leisure Parc
Bonville's Court Cott.
CASTLE VIEW
WHITLOW
Caravan Park
Caravan Park

The Valley
RIDGEWAY CL.
WHITLOW
Scar Farm
STRANDWAY

Rainbows End
INCLINE WAY
Bonville's Court (site)
RIDGEWAY WAY
VANDERHOOF WAY
Saundersfoot Prim. Sch.
MONKSTONE VIEW
THE STRAND

THE INCLINE
FRANCES TER.
CHURCH ST.
FRANCES LA.
BEACH CT.
Front Beach

The Back
WESTFIELD ROAD
PENNANT AV.
ROSEWOOD COTTS.
HIGH ST.
CAMBRIAN PL.
WIGAN TER.
HOLME EK.
FRANCES RD.

Camping Site
THE INCLINE
MILFORD
LANTERN CT.
Saundersfoot Bay
Slipway

Foxen Holes
BROOKLAND PL.
BROOKLAND
Lib. & Regency Hall
HARBOUR
BREWERY TER.
Sailing Club
Harbour-master's Office Harbour

Saundersfoot
Little Griffithston
King George's Field
Football Grd.
Caravan Park
BOWER
CAPTAINS WALK
Steps to beach
Back Beach

Castle Pretty
Griffithston Farm
Fb.
RAGGED STAFF
HILL COTTS.
MALIN CT.
ST. BRIDES HILL
RAINBOW VALE

Upper Hopshill Cottage
Woodside Cottage
Fb.
RAGGED STAFF
LAWNSWOOD CT.
STRATHCLYDE CT.
FRANCES COTTS.
ST. BRIDES LANE
STAMMERS ROAD
THE DINGLE
GREENLEA

Lower Hopshill Farm
Griffithston Hall
SANDY HILL PK.
BEVELIN HALL
BEVELIN COTTS.
HALL
The Plantation
Rhosneath
The Glen
Glen Beach

Braymore
SANDY HILL
BEVELIN
SWALLOW DW.
SCANDANAVIA HTS.
REGENTS
SCANDANAVIA
BEVELIN
Rhode Wood

Bethesda
Hopshill Mountain Farm
HILLSIDE COTTS.
HILL
Rusheylake
RUSHEY
GWENMOL
GWENOL
Caravan Park

The Leys
To Tenby
SANDY HILL ROAD
Saundersfoot Bay Leisure Park
Rusheylake Bridge
B4316
BROOMFIELD
Dangoed's Wood
HILL
GWENNEL CWM.

E   **F**   **G**   **H**

A4310
GWENDRAETH RD.
HEOL HIRWAUN OLAU
Opencast Coal Workings
Tumble

32
Hall
HEOL Y NEUADD
Dismantled Railway
Quarries (dis)

64
RHOSNEWYDD
60
Shaft (dis)
LLECHYFEDACH
HEOL BRYNGWILI
A476 To Cross Hands

30
Sch.
Llechyfedach Prim. Sch.
ROAD

Maesgwern
MAESGWERN
RAILWAY PENPARC
Tumble (Y Tymbl)
KEW GDNS.
Bryncoch
Upper Tumble

Factory
Playing Field
RAILWAY
HEOL Y BRYN ST.
95 50 51
BETHANIA

28
Oakland
Burial Grnd.
Singleton Rd.
Playgrd.

swenllian
TYISHA ROAD
TIR BECA
Bryntawel
DARREN LAS

Ty'n-y-waun
Afon Goch
Ty-isaf
Fire & Amb. Stn.

Lletty-mawr
A476 LLANNON RD.
TROED Y BRYN
BANC Y BRYN

Tynewydd
LLETY ROAD
GORS ROAD
To Lianelli

Pant-y-ffynnon
ntled Railway
Garnfâch

E   **F**   **G**   **H**

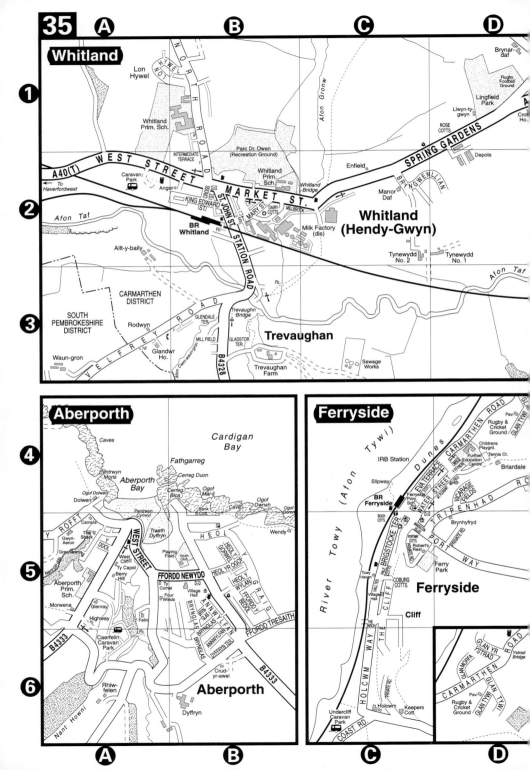

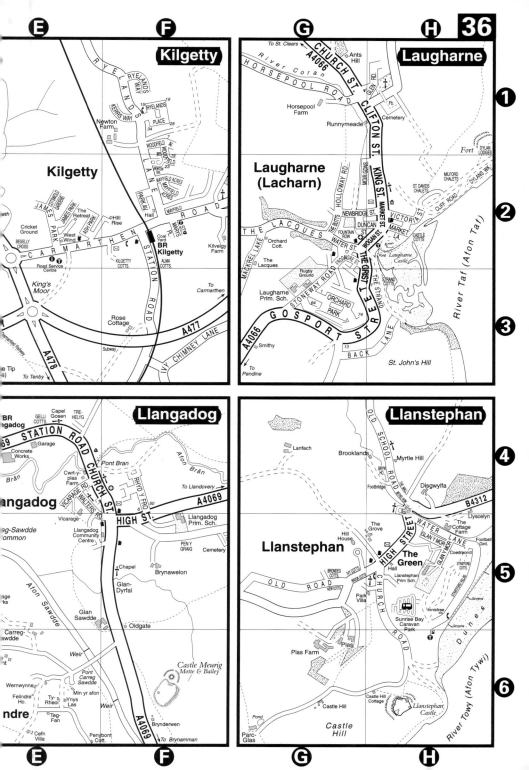

Kilgetty

Laugharne

Llangadog

Llanstephan

Kilgetty

Laugharne
(Lacharn)

Llanstephan

The
Green

E F G H

1
2
3
4
5
6

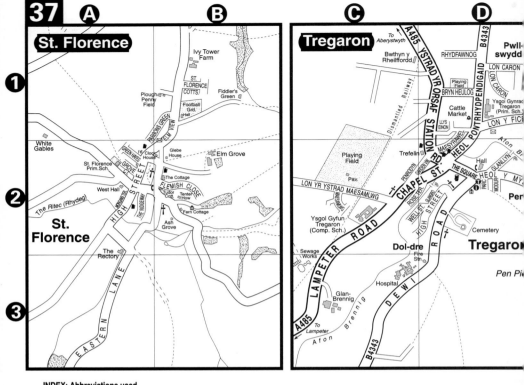

A   **B**   **C**   **D**

St. Florence

Tregaron

INDEX: Abbreviations used

App.	Approach	Cott(s).	Cottage(s)	Gr.	Grove	Lib.	Library	Rd.	Road
Av.	Avenue	Cres.	Crescent	Grd.	Ground	Lit.	Little	S.	South
Bldgs.	Buildings	Ct.	Court	Grn.	Green	Mark.	Market	Sch.	School
Br.	Bridge	Dis.	Disused	Gt.	Great	Mt.	Mount	Sq.	Square
Bus.	Business	Dr.	Drive	Ho.	House	N.	North	St.	Street
Cara.	Caravan	E.	East	Hosp.	Hospital	Pav.	Pavilion	Stn.	Station
Cem.	Cemetery	Ent.	Enterprise	Ind.	Industrial	Pk.	Park	Ter.	Terrace
Cl.	Close	Est.	Estate	Inf.	Infant	Pl.	Place	Up.	Upper
Comm.	Community	Fb.	Footbridge	Junc.	Junction	Prim.	Primary	W.	West
Comp.	Comprehensive	Gdns.	Gardens	La.	Lane	Rec.	Recreation	Wlk.	Walk

Use of this Index

1. An alphabetical order is followed.
2. Each street name is followed by a map reference giving a page number and coordinates: Albert Street 27 C2.
3. Where a street runs across more than one page the reference number is given: Heol Rheidol 7 D1-8 E1.
4. Where a street name appears more than once the reference is given: Brynglas 35 B5/B6.
5. House numbers along streets are shown: *250*.

MYNEGAI: Byrfoddau a ddefnyddir

App.	Dynesiad	Cott(s).	Bwthyn(bythynnod)	Gr.	Llwyn	Lib.	Llyfrgell	Rd.	Heol
Av.	Rhodfa	Cres.	Cilgant	Grd.	Maes	Lit.	Bach	S.	De
Bldgs.	Adeiladau	Ct.	Llys	Grn.	Maes	Mark.	Marchnad	Sch.	Ysgol
Br.	Pont	Dis.	Nis defnyddir	Gt.	Mawr	Mt.	Mynydd	Sq.	Sgwâr
Bus.	Busnes	Dr.	Rhodfa	Ho.	Ty	N.	Gogledd	St.	Stryd
Cara.	Carafán	E.	Dwyrain	Hosp.	Ysbyty	Pav.	Pafiliwn	Stn.	Gorsaf
Cem.	Mynwent	Ent.	Anturiaeth	Ind.	Diwydiannol	Pk.	Parc	Ter.	Teras
Cl.	Clos	Est.	Ystad	Inf.	Babanod	Pl.	Place	Up.	Uchaf
Comm.	Cymuned	Fb.	Pont i gerddwyr	Junc.	Cyffordd	Prim.	Cynradd	W.	Gorllewin
Comp.	Cyfun	Gdns.	Gerddi	La.	Lôn	Rec.	Hamdden	Wlk.	Rhodfa

Heol Rheidol 7 D1-8 E1.

Sut i ddefnyddio'r

1. Dilynnir trefn yr wyddor.
2. Dilynnir enw pob stryd gan gyfeiriad map yn rhoi rhif tudalen a chyfesurynnau: Albert Street 27 C2.
3. Lle y rhêd stryd dros fwy nag un tudalen rhoddir y cyfeiriad: Heol Rheidol 7 D1-8 E1.
4. Lle ymddengys enw stryd fwy nag unwaith rhoddir y cyfeiriad: Brynglas 35 B5/B6.
5. Dangosir rhifau'r tai ar hyd y strydoedd: *250*.

ABERAERON
Population: 1500
Market Day: Wenesday

Alban Square....27 C1/C2
Albert Street....27 C2
Beach Parade....27 B2
Belle Vue Gardens....27 B1
Belle Vue Terrace....27 B1
Berllan Deg....27 C3
Bridge Street....27 B1
Bro Allt y Graig....27 C1
Bryn Road....27 C1
Bryn y Mor....27 C1
Cadwgan Place....27 B1
Castle Lane....27 C1
Chalybeate Gardens....27 C2
Coed y Bryn....27 C3
Cylch Aeron....27 C2
Dark Gate Street....27 C1
Dol Heulog....27 C2
Drury Lane....27 B1
Ffordd y Goitre....27 C2
Glanafon....27 C2
Greenland Terrace....27 B2
Heol Panteg....27 C1
Lampeter Road....27 C3
Lower Regent Street....27 C1
Market Street....27 C1
Masons Road....27 C1
Newfoundland Terrace....27 B2
North Road....27 C1
Oxford Street....27 C1
Peniel Lane....27 C1
Penmaenglas....27 B2
Portland Place....27 C2
Princes Avenue....27 C1
Quay Parade....27 B1
Queen Street....27 C1
Regent Street....27 C1
Ship Street....27 B1
South Road....27 C2
Spring Gardens....27 C3
Tabernacle Street....27 B1
Vicarage Road....27 C3
Victoria Street....27 C1
Vulcan Road....27 B1
Water Street....27 C2
Waterloo Street....27 B1
Wellington Street....27 B1

ABERPORTH
Population: 1450

Annwylfan....35 B5/B6
Brynglas....35 B5/B6
Dyffryn Terrace....35 B6
Ffordd Newydd....35 B5
Ffordd Tresaith....35 B6
Ffordd y Bedol....35 B5
Heol y Gorwel....35 B5
Heol y Graig....35 B5
Heol y Wylan....35 B5
Heol yr Ogof....35 B5
West Street....35 A5
Y Ddol....35 A5
Y Rofft....35 A5

ABERYSTWYTH
Population: 11270
Market Day: Monday

Albert Place....7 B1
Alexandra Road....7 B2
Alfred Place....7 B2
Antaron Avenue....7 D6
Baker Street....7 B2
Banadl Road....7 C2
Beehive Terrace....7 B4
Bilston Terrace....8 E4
Brewer Street....7 B2
Bridge Street....7 B3
Bridgend Cottages....7 B3
Broadway....7 D4
Brongwinau....8 G1
Brook Terrace....8 E4
Bryn Ceinion....8 F2
Bryn Hendre....8 E1
Bryn Rheidol....8 E4
Bryn Ystwyth....7 C5
Bryn y Mor Road....7 B1
Bryn y Mor Terrace....7 B1
Brynglas Road....7 D3
Cae Melyn....7 B4
Cae Rope Walk....7 B4
Caer Gog....7 C2
Cambrian Place....7 B2
Cambrian Square....7 C2
Cambrian Street....7 B2
Cambridge Terrace....7 B2
Caradoc Road....7 C2
Castle Street....7 A2
Castle Terrace....7 A3
Cathedral View....7 D3
Cefn Llan....8 E3
Cefnesgair....8 F3
Chalybeate Street....7 B2
Clawdd Helyg....8 G1
Cliff Road....7 B1
Cliff Terrace....7 B1
Cogerddan Cottages....7 C2
Corporation Street....7 B2
Custom House Street....7 A3
Cwrt yr Onnen....8 E4
Cynfryn Buildings....7 B2
Dan y Coed....7 C2
Dinas Terrace....7 B4
Eastgate Street....7 B2
Edge Hill Road....7 C2
Elm Tree Avenue....7 B2
Elysian Grove....7 C2
Erw Goch....8 F2
Felin y Mor Road....7 A5
Ffordd Pant y Rhos....8 E2
Ffordd Sulien....8 E4
Fifth Avenue....7 C4
First Avenue....7 C5
Fourth Avenue....7 C5
Garth Dinas....7 D6
George Street....7 B3
Gerddi Rheidol....7 A4
Glanrafon Terrace....7 B3
Glanyrafon Industrial Estate....8 G5
Glyndwr Road....7 B3
Grays Inn Road....7 B3
Great Darkgate Street....7 B2
Green Gardens....7 B3
Greenfield Street....7 B3
Harbour Crescent....7 B3
Haulwen....7 C5
Heol Alun....8 E2
Heol Bryn....7 D5
Heol Dinas....7 D5
Heol Isaf....7 C4
Heol Iwain....8 E4
Heol Nanteos....7 C5
Heol Rheidol....7 D1-8 E1
Heol Tyn y Fron....7 D5
Heol Ystrad....7 C5
Heol y Bont....7 D5
Heol y Bryn....7 B1
Heol y Buarth....7 C2
Heol y Garth....7 C5
Heol y Llan....8 E4
Heol y Wern....7 C5
High Street....7 B3
Infirmary Road....7 C2
Iorwerth Avenue....7 C2
King Street....7 A2
Kings Crescent....7 D3
Laura Place....7 A2
Laurel Place....7 B2
Lewis Terrace....8 E4
Lisburne Terrace....7 B2
Llanbadarn Industrial Estate....8 E4
Llanbadarn Road....7 C3/8 F4
Lluest Mews....8 F3
Llwyn yr Eos....7 D6
Llys Hendre....8 E2
Llys Mynach....8 E1
Lon Cleddau....7 D1
Lon Conwy....8 E1
Lon Dyfi....8 E1
Lon Hendre....8 E1
Lon Teifi....8 E1
Lon Ystwyth....8 E1
Loveden Cottages....8 G1
Loveden Road....8 F2
Maes Ceinion....8 F2
Maes Cogerddan....7 C2
Maes Maelor....7 C5
Maes y Ffynnon....7 C5
Maesheli....7 C5
Maeshendre....8 E2
Maesyrafon....7 B3
Marine Terrace....7 B2
Market Street....7 B2
Mill Street....7 B3
Min y Ddol....7 C5
Moor Lane....7 B2
New Promenade....7 A2/A4
New Street....7 A2
North Parade....7 B2
North Road....7 B1
Northgate Street....7 C2
Norton Terrace....7 C3
Orchard, The....7 C5
Padarn Crescent....7 D3
Padarn Lane....8 E4
Padarn Terrace....8 E4
Parc Dolau....7 C5
Park Avenue....7 B3
Pen y Fron Cottages....8 E3
Pen y Fron Road....8 E4
Pen y Graig....7 C1
Pendre Cottages....8 F4
Penglais Farm Cottages....8 E1
Penglais Road....7 C2/8 F1
Penglais Terrace....7 C2
Penmaes Glas....7 A3
Penparcau Road....7 B4/C5
Pentre Jane Morgan Student Village....8 E1
Penygraig....8 E4
Penygraig Court....7 C2
Pier Street....7 B2
Plas Avenue....7 D3
Plas Dan y Coed....7 C2
Plas Helyg....7 C4
Plas Helyg Avenue....7 C5
Plas Morolwg....7 B4
Plascrug Avenue....7 C3
Poplar Row....7 C2
Portland Road....7 B2
Portland Street....7 B2
Pound Place....7 C2
Powell Street....7 B3
Primrose Hill....8 E3
Princess Street....8 E3
Prospect Place....8 E4
Prospect Street....7 A3
Pwllhobi....8 E4
Pwllhobi Terrace....8 E4
Quay Road....7 A3
Quebec Row....7 D4
Queen Street....7 B3
Queens Avenue....7 B1
Queens Road....7 B1/B2
Rheidol Close....7 D5
Rheidol Place....7 B3
Rheidol Road....7 C5
Rheidol Terrace....7 A3
Rheidol View....7 C5
Rhos Hendre....8 E2
Rhybudd Student Village....8 E2
Rhydybont....7 C5
Rhydyr Afon....7 B3
Riverside Terrace....7 B3
Sea View Place....7 A3
Second Avenue....7 C5
Skinner Street....7 C2
South Marine Terrace....7 A3
South Road....7 B2
Spring Gardens....7 B3
St. Davids Road....7 C2
St. Davids Wharf Flats....7 A4
St. Georges Terrace....7 D4
St. James Square....7 B3
St. Johns Flats....7 B2
St. Johns Square....7 A4
St. Michaels Place....7 A3
Stanley Road....7 C2
Stanley Terrace....7 B2
Swan Square....7 B2
Terrace Road....7 B2
Thespian Street....7 B2
Third Avenue....7 C5
Trefaenor....8 H2
Trefechan Road....7 B3
Trefor Road....7 C2
Trinity Place....7 C2
Trinity Road....7 C2
Tyn y Fron Road....7 D6
Tyn y Fron Lane....7 D6
Union Street....7 B2
Vaenor Street....7 B2
Victoria Terrace....7 B1
Vulcan Street....7 A3
Waterside Apartments....7 B3
Waun Fawr Cottages....8 E2
William Street....7 B3
Ystwyth Close....7 D5

AMMANFORD
Population: 10190

Aberlash Road....9 C1
Ammanford Road....9 A6/10 H5
Argoed Road....10 E6
Arthur Street....9 D2
Ashgrove....10 G3
Bancgeredig....10 H3
Baptist Lane....10 E4
Betws Industrial Park....10 F3
Betws Road....10 E5
Bishop Road....9 D4
Bonllwyn....9 D1
Brodawell....10 F5
Bryn Derwen Road....9 D2
Bryn Euraidd....9 C4
Bryn Hafod (Tycroes)....9 A6/10 H5
Bryn Teg Terrace....9 D3
Brynmawr Avenue....9 D2-10 E3
Brynmawr Lane....10 E5
Caemawr....10 E5
Carregamman....9 D4-10 E4
Carregamman Isaf....10 F5
Carregamman Lane....10 E3
Church Street....10 E3
College Street....9 D2
Colonel Road....10 E3
Cwm Saeson (Tycroes)....10 G5
Derlin Park (Tycroes)....10 G6
Dyffryn Road....9 A3-C3
Dynevor Cottages....9 C6
Fairoak....10 G2
Farm Road....10 G2
Fferws Road (Tycroes)....10 G5
Ffordd y Afon....9 D1
Florence Road....9 D2
Forest Fach Estate....9 B6
Foundry Road....10 E4
Foundry Row....10 E4
Gellywreiddon Road (Tycroes)....9 A5/10 H4
Hafod Road (Tycroes)....9 A6/10 H5
Hall Street....10 E3
Harold Street....9 D3
Hendre Road (Tycroes)....10 G4
Heol Brown (Tycroes)....9 A6/10 H5
Heol Ddu (Tycroes)....10 G6
Heol Hayden....9 C2
Heol Las....9 D4
Heol Llwchwr....9 D5
Heol Llwyd....9 D1
Heol Marlais....9 D2
Heol Wallasey....10 E4
Heol y Felin....10 E5
Heol y Wyrddol....9 D2
High Street....10 E3
Iscennen Road....9 D3
James Griffiths Road....10 G3
Laurel Drive....10 G3
Llandybie Road....9 D1
Lloyd Street....10 E3
Llwyn Maes....9 D1
Llwyn y Bryn....9 D1
Lon Ger y Coed....10 H3
Lon y Gruglas (Tycroes)....9 A5/10 H4
Maerdy Road....10 E6
Maes Quarre Road....10 G3
Maes y Berllan....10 E6
Maes y Coed....10 H3
Maes y Dail....9 B3
Maes yr Haf....9 B3
Manor Road....9 D3
Margaret Street....10 E3
Mill Terrace....10 E6
Myddynfych Drive....9 D1
Mynydd Bach (Tycroes)....10 G5
Nant Lais....9 D2
New Road....9 D5
Newtown....9 B4
Norman Road....9 D2
Oakfield Terrace....10 F3
Old Road....9 D2
Pant y Betws....10 E5
Pantyfynnon Road....9 C6
Parc Amanwy....9 D5
Parc Bwtrmawr....10 E5
Parc Henry Lane....9 D1
Parc Pen Rhiw....10 E6
Parcyrhun....9 D5
Park Mill Road....9 B4
Park Street....10 E4
Parklands Road....9 B3
Pen y Banc Road....9 A5-D4/10 H4
Pen y Fan....10 F2
Pentwyn Road....10 F3
Penydre Estate....10 F3
Penygam Road (Tycroes)....10 G6
Pinewood Road....10 G3
Plas y Coed....9 C6
Pont Amman Road....10 G3
Pontardulais Rd. (Tycroes)....10 G6
Quay Street....10 E3
Rhodfa Frank....9 C2
Rhos Terrace (Tycroes)....10 G5
Rice Street....10 E3
School Lane....10 E3
Shands Road....9 B1/C2
Station Road....9 C2
Stewart Drive....9 D3
Talbot Road....9 D3
Tegfan....9 D2
Teglan Park (Tycroes)....10 G6
Tir Prys (Tycroes)....9 A6/10 H5
Tir y Dail Lane....9 D3
Treforis....10 E6
Trefrhiw Road....9 B4
Union Street....9 D4
Villiers Road....9 D4
Walter Road....10 F3
Waun Fawr....9 B3
Wern Ddu Road....10 F2
Wernoleu Road....10 G3
Wind Street....9 D4
Woodfield Terrace....10 H3

BRYNAMMAN
Population: 1650

Amman Cottages....27 B6
Amman Road....27 C5
Ardwyn Road....27 C5
Arfryn....27 C4
Banwen Place....27 A6
Bryn Avenue....27 B5
Bryn Bach Road....27 A5
Bryn Road....27 B4
Brynceunant....27 C4
Bungalows, The....27 B6
Castell Road....27 B6
Chapel Street....27 B5
Coronation Road....27 C4
Cwmgarw Road....27 A5
Esgairynys....27 A5
Glyn Road....27 A6
Groesffordd....27 B5
Hall Street....27 B5
Heol Gelynen....27 B5
Heol Godfrey....27 A6
Llandeilo Road....27 A5-B5
Maes y Deri....27 A6
Maes y Glyn....27 A6
Mountain Road....27 C5
New Road....27 C5
Park Road....27 A6
Park Street....27 A6
Quarry Road....27 B4
Rhosfa Road....27 D4
School Street....27 A6
Station Road....27 B6

CARDIGAN
ABERTEIFI
Population: 3850
Market Day: Saturday

Aberystwyth Road....19 B5
Alltfach....19 C1
Baptist Street....19 C1
Bath House....19 B4
Bath House Road....19 B4
Brecon Terrace....19 C4
Bridge Street....19 C4
Bro Teifi....19 C5
Bron y Dre....19 B4
Brondesbury Lodge....19 A6
Brooklyn Villas....19 B5
Bryn Hafod....19 B5
Bryngwyn....19 D2
Brynhyfryd....19 C1
Cambrian Terrace....19 C2
Carriers Lane....19 C4

Temple Terrace ... 28 F5
Tregaron Road ... 28 F4
Victoria Terrace ... 28 F6

LAUGHARNE
LACHARN
Population: 1272

Back Lane ... 36 G3
Butts, The ... 36 G2
Castle Cottages ... 36 H2
Church Street ... 36 G1
Cliff Road ... 36 H2
Clifton Street ... 36 H1
Duncan Street ... 36 G2
Dylan Lodges ... 36 H1
Dylans Walk ... 36 H2
Fountain Row ... 36 G2
Frogmore Street ... 36 G2
Glen Road ... 36 H1
Gosport Street ... 36 G3
Grist, The ... 36 G2
Holloway Road ... 36 G2
Horsepool Road ... 36 G1
King Street ... 36 H2
Laques, The ... 36 G2
Mackrel Lake ... 36 G3
Market Lane ... 36 H2
Market Street ... 36 H2
Milford Chalets ... 36 H3
Moir Gardens ... 36 G2
Newbridge Street ... 36 G2
Orchard Park ... 36 G3
St. Davids Chalets ... 36 H2
Stoneway Road ... 36 G3
Strand Cottages ... 36 H3
Strand, The ... 36 H3
Victoria Street ... 36 H2
Water Street ... 36 G2
Wogan Street ... 36 H2

LLANDEILO
Population: 2410
Market Day: Saturday

Abbey Terrace ... 29 C3
Abernant Cottages ... 29 A1
Alan Road ... 29 C2
Bank Buildings ... 29 C2
Bank Terrace ... 29 B3
Bethlehem Road ... 29 D3
Blende Road ... 29 C2
Bridge Street ... 29 B3
Brisken Terrace ... 29 C2
Brooklands Terrace ... 29 C1
Brynawel Terrace ... 29 B2
Carmarthen Road ... 29 A1
Carmarthen Street ... 29 B2
Church Street ... 29 B3
Cilcennen Terrace ... 29 C1
Clarence Road ... 29 C2
Clarendon Road ... 29 C2
Crescent Road ... 29 C2
Diana Road ... 29 B2
Dirleton Terrace ... 29 C2
Dynevor Avenue ... 29 B2
George Hill ... 29 B3
George Street ... 29 B3
Greenfield Place ... 29 B2
Heol y Garreglas ... 29 C2
King Street ... 29 B3
Latimer Road ... 29 C2
Lewis Terrace ... 29 C2
Lon Rhys ... 29 B1/B2
Maes Elfryn ... 29 B2
Market Street ... 29 B3
New Road ... 29 B3
North Bank ... 29 B2
Parc Lewis ... 29 B2
Quay Street ... 29 B3
Railway Terrace ... 29 C2
Rhosmaen Street ... 29 C2
Sawel Terrace ... 29 C2
Station Road ... 29 C1
Stepney Road ... 29 C2
Thomas Street ... 29 C2
Thomas Terrace ... 29 C2
Wellfield Terrace ... 29 B2
Whitfield Terrace ... 29 B2
Ysgubor Abad ... 29 C3

LLANDOVERY
LLANYMDDYFRI
Population: 1880
Market Day: Friday

Adelaide Street ... 29 C5
Brecon Road ... 29 D5
Bridge Street ... 29 C6
Broad Street ... 29 B6
Castle Street ... 29 C6
Church Bank ... 29 B6
Cilycwm Road ... 29 B4
College View ... 29 B5
Dingat Close ... 29 B5
Dingat Terrace ... 29 B6
Garden Lane ... 29 B6
Gelli Deg ... 29 C5
Heol Rhos ... 29 A4
High Street ... 29 C6
Kings Road ... 29 B6
Llandeilo Road ... 29 A5
Llanfair Road ... 29 B4
Llys Llanfair ... 29 B4
Lon Rhys Pritchard ... 29 B6
Lower Road ... 29 B6
Maes y Coleg ... 29 B5
Maesglas ... 29 C5
Market Square ... 29 B6
New Road ... 29 B5
Orchard Street ... 29 C5
Queen Street ... 29 C5
Queensway ... 29 B5
Railway Terrace ... 29 B5
Rock Cottages ... 29 B6
School Lane ... 29 B5
Stone Street ... 29 B5
Towy Avenue ... 29 B5
Victoria Crescent ... 29 B5
Victoria Street ... 29 C5
Water Street ... 29 C5

LLANDYBIE
Population: 2920
Market Day: Tuesday

Ammanford Road ... 30 F1-G3
Blaenau Road ... 30 F2
Caecoed ... 30 F2/F3
Caeffynnon Road ... 30 G1
Campbell Road ... 30 F1
Church Street ... 30 F1
Derwen Fawr ... 30 G3
Ffordd y Blodau ... 30 G3
Gelly Road ... 30 F2
Glynhir Road ... 30 G3
Heol Ceirios ... 30 G3
Heol Gwilym ... 30 F1
Heol Marlais ... 30 F2
High Street ... 30 F1
Kings Road ... 30 G1
Llandeilo Road ... 30 F1
Maes yr Helyg ... 30 G3
Maespiode ... 30 F2
Maidens Green ... 30 G2
Margaret Road ... 30 F2
Pies Lan ... 30 F1
Rawlings Road ... 30 F2
Woodfield Close ... 30 F2
Woodfield Road ... 30 F2

LLANGADOG
Population: 480

Church Street ... 36 E4
Gelli Cottages ... 36 E4
High Street ... 36 F5
Pen y Graig ... 36 F5
Rhyd y Fro ... 36 F4
Station Road ... 36 E4
Trehelyg ... 36 E4
Vicarage Road ... 36 E4
Walters Road ... 36 E4

LLANSTEPHAN
Population: 480

Bethel Row ... 36 H4
Bethel Terrace ... 36 H4
Brondeg Cottages ... 36 G5
Brook Cottages ... 36 G5
Bryn House ... 36 H4
Church Road ... 36 H5
Glan y Mor ... 36 H5
High Street ... 36 H5
Ivy Cottages ... 36 G5
Mill, The ... 36 H4
New Cottages ... 36 G5
Old Road ... 36 G5
Old School Road ... 36 H4
Stratford Cottages ... 36 H5
Stratford Villas ... 36 H5
Water Lane ... 36 H5

MILFORD HAVEN
Population: 13470
Market Day: Saturday

Albion Street ... 16 E4
Ardent Close ... 16 G3
Ash Grove ... 16 G4
Barlow Street ... 16 E5
Bay View Drive ... 15 B5
Beach Hill ... 16 G5
Blackbridge Crescent ... 16 H5
Brick House ... 16 G6
Bridge Street ... 15 D5
Brooke Avenue ... 16 F5
Bunkers Hill ... 16 G3
Caldy Way ... 16 F3
Camuset Close ... 15 C4
Castle Hall Road ... 16 G5
Castle Pill Crescent ... 16 H2
Castle Pill Road ... 16 H2-H4
Castle Terrace ... 16 F4
Cellar Hill ... 16 G5
Chapel Street ... 16 E6
Charles Street ... 16 E5
Cherry Tree Close ... 16 G4
Chestnut Way ... 16 G4
Church Road ... 15 C4
Clay Lane ... 15 B4
Concrete Cottages ... 16 G6
Conway Drive ... 16 H2
Coombs Drive ... 16 F4
Coombs Road ... 16 G4
Court Rise ... 15 C4
Croft Avenue ... 15 B5
Cromwell Road ... 16 E2-F3
Dairy Park ... 15 D5
Dale Road ... 15 A2-C4
Dartmouth Gardens ... 16 E5
Dartmouth Street ... 16 E5
Derwent Avenue ... 16 H2
Dewsland Street ... 16 E5
Eastleigh Drive ... 16 F5
Edward Street ... 16 E5
Elm Lane ... 16 G4
Exeter Road ... 16 H2
Fairsea Close ... 15 B5
Fold, The ... 16 E1
Francis Street ... 16 F5
Fulke Street ... 16 E5
Gateholm Avenue ... 16 G3
Gelliswick Road ... 15 B6/C5
George Street ... 16 E4
Glastonbury House ... 16 F3
Glebelands ... 15 C5
Gorsewood Drive ... 15 C6
Grassholm Close ... 16 F3
Great North Road ... 16 F5
Green Close ... 16 G2
Green Terrace ... 15 C4
Greville Road ... 16 F5
Grove Housing Estate ... 16 H3
Gwili Road ... 15 D5
Hamilton Terrace ... 16 E5
Harbour Way ... 15 C5
Haven Drive ... 15 B4
Hayston Avenue ... 15 D6
Hill Street ... 15 D5
Hilton Avenue ... 16 G4
Howarth Close ... 16 E3
Imogen Place ... 16 F5
Imperial Terrace ... 16 F4
James Street ... 15 D5
John Lewis Street ... 15 B5
Jordans Close ... 16 H2
Larch Close ... 16 G4
Lawrence Cottages ... 15 C4
Lilac Close ... 16 G3
Linney Way ... 16 F3
Lower Thornton Road ... 16 E1
Lundy Close ... 16 F3
Mable Hall Close ... 16 F4
Mable Hall Road ... 16 F3
Mansfield Street ... 16 F5
Marine Boulevard ... 16 E6
Marine Gardens ... 16 E5
Mariners Way ... 16 H2
Meyler Crescent ... 16 F4
Milford Road ... 16 H1
Milton Crescent ... 16 G5
Milton House ... 16 G5
Monnow Close ... 16 H2
Mount Pleasant Way ... 16 G3
Murray Road ... 16 G6
Nelson Avenue ... 15 D5
Neyland Road (Coombs) ... 16 H5
Neyland Road (Steynton) ... 16 H1
Nubian Crescent ... 15 D6
Oaklands ... 16 G4
Oberon Close ... 16 G2
Observatory Avenue ... 15 C5
Phillips Avenue ... 16 F4
Picton Close ... 15 C5
Picton Road ... 15 C5/C6
Pier Road ... 16 F6
Pill Lane ... 16 F5
Pill Road ... 16 F4
Point Street ... 15 D5/16 E6
Pointfields Crescent ... 15 D6
Pond Meadow ... 16 H2
Prescelly Place ... 16 E4
Priory Lodge Drive ... 16 E4
Priory Lodge Estate ... 16 E4
Priory Road ... 16 E5-F3
Priory Street ... 16 E5
Prioryville ... 16 F4
Ramsey Drive ... 16 F3
Rath, The ... 16 F6
Rectory Avenue ... 15 C5
Richard John Road ... 16 F4
Robert Street ... 16 E5
Roebuck Close ... 16 H2
Romilly Crescent ... 15 D4
Rope Walk, The ... 15 D5
Sandhurst Road ... 16 F6
Shakespeare Avenue ... 16 F5
Sheffield Drive ... 16 H2
Silverstream ... 15 C4
Silverstream Crescent ... 15 D4
Silverstream Drive ... 15 C4
Skomer Drive ... 16 F3
Slaughterhouse Lane ... 16 F5
Slip Hill ... 16 F5
South Hook Road ... 15 A6
Spikes Lane ... 15 D5
St. Annes Drive ... 15 D6
St. Annes Place ... 15 D5
St. Annes Road ... 15 D5
St. Brides Way ... 16 F3
St. Davids Road ... 16 D4
St. Lawrence Avenue ... 15 D5
St. Lawrence Close ... 15 D5
St. Lawrence Hill ... 15 C4-D5
St. Peters Road ... 16 E5
Starbuck Road ... 16 E4
Stephen Street ... 16 E5
Steynton Road ... 16 F4-H2
Stratford Road ... 16 E5
Sycamore Close ... 16 G4
Thornton Housing Estate ... 16 G2
Thornton Industrial Estate ... 16 F2
Thornton Road ... 16 F2
Trafalgar Road ... 16 E5
Upper Hill Street ... 15 D5
Upper Thornton Road ... 16 E1
Vaynor Road ... 16 F4
Vicary Crescent ... 16 G6
Vicary Street ... 16 G6
Victoria Road ... 16 E5
Vivian Drive ... 15 D5
Warrior Road ... 16 H3
Warwick Road ... 16 F5
Waterloo Road ... 15 D5
Wellington Gardens ... 15 D6
Wellington Road ... 15 D5
Wellington Square ... 15 D6
Westaway Drive ... 15 C6
Westfield Drive ... 16 G3
Westhill Avenue ... 16 F4
Willow End ... 16 G4
Windmill Villas ... 15 A5
Woodbine Way ... 15 B4
Woodlands Crescent ... 16 G4
Woodlands Drive ... 16 G4
Yorke Street ... 16 F5

NARBERTH
ARBERTH
Population: 1910
Market Day: Thursday

Adams Drive ... 30 F5
Back Lane ... 30 F5
Belmore Gardens ... 30 F5
Bentley Villas ... 30 G5
Bloomfield Gardens ... 30 F4
Bridge Hill ... 30 F6
Bushes Lane ... 30 F5
Carding Mill Lane ... 30 E5
Castle Street ... 30 F6
Castle Terrace ... 30 F6
Cawdor Court ... 30 F5
Church Street ... 30 F6
Coxhill ... 30 E5
Crescent, The ... 30 F5
Croft Villas ... 30 F5
Drang, The ... 30 F5
Garfield Gardens ... 30 E5
Halkon Crescent ... 30 F5
High Street ... 30 F5
Highfield Park ... 30 E5
Hill Park ... 30 E5
Jesse Road ... 30 F5
Kiln Park Road ... 30 H5
Kings Court ... 30 F5
Market Square ... 30 F5
Market Street ... 30 F5
Mill Lane ... 30 F6
Mill Pond Road ... 30 F6
Millfarm Cottages ... 30 F6
Moorfield ... 30 E5
Moorfield Road ... 30 E4
Nestor Square ... 30 F5
Northfield Court ... 30 F5
Northfield Road ... 30 F5
Northmead ... 30 G5
Parc Roberts ... 30 E4
Park Terrace ... 30 E5
Picton Place ... 30 F5
Picton Terrace ... 30 F5
Queens Street ... 30 F5
Railway Terrace ... 30 H5
Southmead ... 30 G5
Spring Gardens ... 30 F5
Springfield Park ... 30 G4
St. James Street ... 30 F5
Station Approach ... 30 H5
Station Road ... 30 G5/H5
Tabernacle Lane ... 30 F5
Valley Road ... 30 E6
Water Street ... 30 F5
Wells Road Terrace ... 30 E5
Westfield Court ... 30 E5
Williams Court ... 30 F4

NEWCASTLE EMLYN
Population: 1440
Market Day: Friday

Aber Arad Road ... 31 C
Ardwyn Terrace ... 31 B
Blaenwern ... 31 B
Bridge Street ... 31 B
Bryn Deri Close ... 31 B
Bryn Farm Road ... 31 A
Cardigan Road ... 31 A
Carmarthen Road ... 31 D
Castle Road ... 31 B
Castle Terrace ... 31 B
Cawdor Terrace ... 31 B
Coedmor Lane ... 31 B
Coedmor Terrace ... 31 B
College Street ... 31 B
Cwm Cych Road ... 31 A
Cwm Sarah Road ... 31 A
Derby Lane ... 31 B
Derwen Gardens ... 31 B
Ebenezer Street ... 31 B
Emlyn Square ... 31 B
Emlyn Villas ... 31 C
Ffinant Square ... 31 B
Garregwen ... 31 B
Glaspant Terrace ... 31 C
Glazer Row ... 31 B
Heol y Ffinant ... 31 B
Heol y Gof ... 31 B
High Street ... 31 B
Llandyfriog Road ... 31 B2-D
Lloyds Terrace ... 31 B
Maes Llewelyn ... 31 B
Market Place ... 31 B
Market Square ... 31 B
Mill Street ... 31 C
New Road ... 31 A
Old Carmarthen Road ... 31 C
Old Graig Street ... 31 B
Parc Johnson ... 31 B
Parc y Trapp ... 31 B

Woodside Av. (Pembroke) 18 H6

PEN-Y-GROES, CAPEL HENDRE & SARON
Population: 3180

Banc y Ddraenen 25 A5
Black Lion Road.....................25 A4
Blaenau Road 25 C1
Bridge Street 25 A1
Bryn Road 25 A2
Brynawelon 25 D3
Bryncwar Road.......................25 A2
Bryndedwynddfa 25 A2
Brynteg 25 B6
Caer Bryn Road...............25 A2-C1
Caer Bryn Terrace.................25 B1
Cefn Cruc 25 C4
Clos y Cwm 25 A4
Clos yr Hendre 25 B5
Coopers Road 25 B6
Cwm Saeson..........................25 D6
Dyffryn Road 25 D5
Fferws Road 25 D5
Garnfoel 25 A3
Gate Road 25 A1
Glan Rhyd 25 B5
Gors Ddu Road 25 A2
Hendre Road 25 B6-D6
Llwyn Celyn 25 B5
Lotwen Road 25 A6
Maesglas 25 B3
Nant y Ci Road.......................25 D4
Norton Road 25 A1
Park Avenue 25 A5
Penygroes Road 25 B1
Plas Gwyn Road 25 A1
Pontblodau Road 25 D2
Rhos Terrace 25 D6
Saron Road 25 D3
Saron Street 25 B5-D4
Spien Road 25 A3
St. Davids Way 25 A3
Tanyfan 25 B5
Tre Elfred...............................25 B2
Waterloo Road 25 A2-B5
Waterloo Terrace 25 A5

PONTYBEREM
Population: 2620

Ashgrove 24 G5
Bragdu 24 F6
Brandyway 24 F4
Caersalem Row 24 F4
Coalbrook Road......................24 G5
Dreonen 24 G5
Ffordd Aneurin.......................24 F3
Furnace Terrace 24 F5
Greenfield Terrace 24 E5
Grugos Avenue 24 F5
Gwendraeth Row 24 G5
Haulfryn 24 E2
Heol Aneddfa 24 F5
Heol Capel Ifan 24 G4/H3
Heol Llethryd 24 G4
Heol y Banc.....................24 E2-F3
Heol y Bryn 24 E5
Heol y Felin....................24 F3-G4
Heol y Parc 24 G4
Heol y Pentre 24 G4
Hewlett Road 24 G4
Llanon Road 24 G4
Llwynyeos 24 F3
Maesyderi 24 F6
Maesyfelin 24 F4
Min y Graig 24 E5
Mynachog Terrace 24 F5
New Road 24 F5
Parc y Mynach 24 E1
Penybryn 24 E1
Railway Terrace 24 G4
Station Road 24 F6

SAUNDERSFOOT
Population: 2680

Bath Cottages 34 G3
Bedoes Court 34 H2
Belle View 34 G1
Bench Court 34 H1
Bevelin Hall 34 G3
Bevelyn Lane 34 H3
Brewery Cottages 34 H2
Brewery Flats 34 H2
Brewery Terrace 34 H2

Brookland Close......................34 H2
Brookland Place......................34 H2
Broomfield Hill.......................34 G3
Cambrian Place 34 H2
Captains Walk 34 H2
Cartref 34 G1
Castle View 34 G1
Chestnut Cottages 34 G1
Church Terrace 34 H1
Coedrath Park.........................34 G1
Cwm Gwennol.........................34 H3
Dingle, The.............................34 H3
Fan Road, The.........................34 F1
Frances Cottages 34 G2
Frances Lane 34 G1
Frances Road 34 H1
Garden Cottage Flats 34 G1
Glenvale 34 H3
Guys Villas 34 G1
Harbour Court 34 H2
Harbour Heights 34 H2
Hean Close 34 G1
High Street 34 H1
Hill Cottages 34 H1
Hillside Cottages 34 G3
Holmlea Court 34 H1
Incline Way 34 F1/G2
Incline, The 34 F1
Lantern Court 34 H2
Lawnswood 34 G2
Malin Court 34 G2
Milford Street 34 H2
Milford Terrace 34 H1
Monkstone View 34 H1
Nash Place 34 G1
North Close.............................34 F1
Nyth Gwennol 34 G3
Pennant Avenue 34 G1
Plantation Cottages 34 G3
Ragged Staff...........................34 G2
Rainbow Vale 34 H2
Rhodewood Terrace................34 H3
Ridgeway Close.......................34 H1
Ridgeway, The.........................34 F1
Rose Mount 34 G1
Rosewood Cottages 34 G1
Rushey Lane 34 G3
Sandy Hill Park 34 G3
Sandy Hill Road.......................34 F3
Scandanavia Heights..............34 G3
St. Brides Gardens..................34 H3
St. Brides Hill 34 H1
St. Brides Lane........................34 G2
Stammers Road.......................34 G2
Stathclyde Court 34 H2
Strand, The.............................34 H1
Strandway Court 34 H1
Swallow Dale 34 G3
Valley Road.............................34 E1
Vanderhoof Way......................34 G1
Westfield Court 34 G1
Westfield Road........................34 G1
White Park Bungalows 34 F1
Whitlow 34 G1
Windsor Terrace 34 H1
Wogan Lane............................34 H1
Wogan Terrace 34 H1

ST. CLEARS
SANCLER
Population: 1800

Bridge Street 33 C3
Brittannia Terrace 33 B2
Brynawel.................................33 A1
Carmarthen Road 33 D2
Clare Hill 33 A1
Corvus Terrace 33 D2
Craig Villas 33 C3
Croft Cottages 33 C3
Gelli 33 A3
Gerddi Mair Estate 33 C2
Gors Fach 33 A1
Heol Gerig 33 A3
Heol Goi 33 C3
High Street 33 C2
Kieff Park Terrace 33 C3
Kingswood Terrace 33 D1
Llwyn Du 33 A1
Llysalaw..................................33 A1
Lon Hafren 33 D1
Lon Prior 33 C1
Lonlas 33 A1

Pandy Grove 33 C2
Parcglas 33 B2
Pentre Road............................33 C2
Spring Gardens 33 A1
Springfield 33 C1
Station Road 33 D1
Tenby Road.............................33 B2
Tir Owen.................................33 C1
Ysgubor Fawr 33 A1

ST.DAVID'S
TY DDEWI
Population: 1460

Bryn Road 33 B5
Bryn Teg.................................33 B6
Catherine Street 33 B5
Cross Square 33 B5
Feidr Pant y Bryn 33 C6
Feidr Treginnis 33 A5
Ffordd Caerfai 33 C6
Ffordd Melin Isaf 33 A6
Ffordd Porth Clais 33 A6
Ffos y Mynach.........................33 B6
Ffynnon Wen 33 B6
Goat Street 33 B5
Gospel Lane 33 B5
Heol Dewi 33 C5
High Street 33 C5
Maes Dewi 33 C5
Maes Dyfed.............................33 C5
Maes y Dre 33 C5
Maes y Hedydd 33 C4
Meidr Dwyll.............................33 C4
Millard Park 33 C5
Mitre Lane 33 B5
New Street 33 C5
Noddfa Dewi...........................33 C5
Nun Street 33 B5
Pebbles, The 33 B5
Pen Rhiw................................33 B4
Pen y Garn 33 B5
Peters Lane 33 C5
Pigfoot Lane 33 B5
Pit Street 33 B5
Quickwell Hill 33 B4
St. Nons Close 33 B5
Steps Lane 33 B5
Tower Hill...............................33 B5
Town Hall Lane 33 C5
Waun Isaf 33 A6
Yr Hafon.................................33 B5

ST. FLORENCE
Population: 470

Eastern Lane 37 A3
Elm View.................................37 B1
Flemish Close.........................37 B2
Green Hayes 37 A2
Grove Court 37 A2
High Street 37 A2
Morgans Terrace 37 A2
Parsons Green 37 B1
Ridgeway, The.........................37 A2
St. Florence Cotts. 37 B1

TENBY
DINBYCH-Y-PYSGOD
Population: 5630
Market Days: Wednesday & Saturday

Alma Flats (Penally) 26 H6
Alma Gardens (Penally) 26 G6
Augustus Place 26 G3
Battery Road...........................26 G2
Blind Lane 26 F1/F2
Bridge Street 26 H3
Broadwell Hayes 26 F2
Brynhir Cottages 26 F1
Cambrian Cottages 26 F2
Castle Square 26 H3
Church Park 26 G4
Church Street 26 G4
Churchill Close 26 E3
Clareston Road 26 G3
Clement Terrace 26 G3
Clicketts Lane 26 E3
Clicketts, The..........................26 E3
Cob Lane.................................26 H4
Crackwell Street 26 G3
Cresswell Street 26 G4
Croft Court 26 G2
Croft, The 26 G3
Culver Park 26 G4

Deer Park 26 G3
Edward Street 26 G4
Esplanade 26 G6
Gas Lane 26 G2
Giltar Terrace (Penally).........26 H6
Glas Nevin Gardens 26 F2
Glebe, The..............................26 G2
Glen View Crescent 26 F2
Green, The 26 F3
Greenhill Avenue 26 G3
Greenhill Road 26 G3
Harding Street 26 G4
Harries Street 26 G4
Heywood Court.......................26 F2
High Street 26 G3
Hill Cottages (Penally) 26 G6
Hill Farm Road (Penally).......26 G6
Hill Park 26 F2
Holloway Court (Penally) 26 H5
Holloway Hill (Penally)..........26 G5
Hoyles Close (Penally) 26 H5
Ivy Cottages 26 H4
Jubilee Cottages 26 F2
Kenystyle (Penally) 26 H5
Knowling Mead.......................26 E3
Lady Park 26 F1/F2
Lamark Vale 26 G4
Laxton Flats 26 H3
Leach Way 26 F2
Lexden Terrace 26 H4
Lower Frog Street 26 G4
Lower Park Road.....................26 F3
Marsh Road.............................26 E3
Marsh Road Cottages 26 F3
Maudlins 26 G4
Merlins Court 26 G3
Middle Walls Lane (Penally) ...26 H5
Narberth Road 26 F1-G2
Nelson Walk 26 F3
Newell Hill..............................26 G3
Newood Lane 26 E3
North Walk 26 G4
Norton 26 G2
Oakridge Acres.......................26 E3
Paddock, The 26 F2
Paragon 26 H4
Paragon Court 26 H4
Park Place 26 G4
Park Road 26 G4
Park Terrace 26 G4
Penally Hill 26 G4
Penally Road...........................26 G3
Picton Road 26 G4
Picton Terrace 26 G4
Pier Hill..................................26 H3
Quarry Cottages 26 G4
Quay Hill.................................26 H3
Queens Parade 26 G4
Queensfield 26 E3
Rectory Court 26 G3
Regency Court 26 G3
Ritec Row (Penally) 26 H5
Rock Terrace 26 H4
Rocky Park 26 G4
Rosemount Garden Villas 26 F3
Rosemount Gardens 26 F3
Saltern Industrial Estate 26 F4
Serpentine Road 26 F3
Silven Flats 26 G2
Slippery Back 26 F3
South Parade 26 G4
Southcliffe Street 26 G4
Southlands 26 G4
Sperricomb Lane 26 F1
St. Catherines Flats 26 H3
St. Davids Close 26 E3
St. Florence Green 26 G4
St. Georges Street 26 G4
St. Johns Hill 26 G3
St. Julians Street 26 H3
St. Julians Terrace 26 H3
St. Marys Street 26 G4
St. Nicholas Cres. (Penally) ...26 H5
Station Road 26 G4
Strawberry Gardens (Pen.).....26 H6
Strawberry Lane (Penally) 26 G6
Sutton Street 26 G4
Trafalgar Road........................26 G4
Tudor Square 26 H3
Tudor Way 26 E3
Upper Frog Street 26 G3

Upper Hill Park 26 F2
Upper Park Road.....................26 G3
Victoria Cottages 26 G4
Victoria Street 26 G4
Wallsfield 26 G3
Warren Street 26 G3
Waterwynch Lane 26 G1
Weston Terrace 26 G3
White Lion Street 26 G4
Zion Gardens 26 G3

TREGARON
Population: 870
Market Day: Tuesday

Bryn Heulog 37 D1
Chapel Street 37 D1
Dewi Road...............................37 C3
Gardens View..........................37 D2
Glangro...................................37 D1
Glanllyn 37 D2
Heol Pontrhydpendigaid 37 D2
Heol y Mynydd 37 D2
High Street 37 C3
Lampeter Road 37 C3
Llys Einon...............................37 D1
Lon Caron 37 D1
Lon y Ficerdy 37 C1
Lon yr Ystrad Maesamlwg 37 C2
Maesamlwg.............................37 C2
Maesyrawel 37 D2
Parc Modur 37 D2
Penrodyn 37 D1
Rhydfawnog 37 D1
Rose Terrace 37 D2
Square, The 37 D2
Station Road 37 C1
Well Street 37 D1
Ystrad yr Orsaf.......................37 D1

TUMBLE
Y TYMBL
Population: 2840

Banc y Gors 34 G6
Bethania Road 34 G5-H4
Bethesda Road 34 E5-F4
Darren Las 34 G6
Derwen Road...........................34 F4
Gors Road...............................34 G4
Gwendraeth Road 34 E4
Heol Bryngwili 34 F4
Heol Hirwaun Olau..................34 F4
Heol y Bryn 34 F4
Heol y Neuadd.........................34 F4
High Street 34 H5
Kew Gardens 34 H5
Llannon Road 34 G6
Llechyfedach 34 H4
Llety Road 34 G6
Maesgwern 34 H4
Penparc 34 F5
Railway Place 34 F5
Railway Terrace 34 F5
Rhosnewydd 34 E4
Singleton Road 34 G5
Station View 34 G4
Tir Beca 34 F4
Troedy Bryn 34 G6
Tyisha Road 34 F5

WHITLAND
HENDY-GWYN
Population: 1470
Market Day: Friday

Bryngwenllian..........................35 C2
Cross Street 35 B2
Dairy Cottages.........................35 B2
Gladstor Terrace 35 B1
Glendale Terrace 35 B2
Intermediate Terrace...............35 B2
King Edward Street 35 A1
Lon Hywel 35 A1
Market Street 35 B2
Millbrook 35 B2
Millfield 35 A3
North Road..............................35 B1
Rose Cottages 35 C2
Spring Gardens 35 C2
St. Johns Street.......................35 B2
St. Mary Street 35 B2
Station Road 35 B2
Velfrey Road...........................35 A3
West Street 35 B1